# THEMATIC UNIT
# FOOD

*Written by Lola Willrich*

*Edited by Karen J. Goldfluss*

*Illustrated by Sue Fullam, Cheryl Buhler, and Blanca Apodaca*

*Teacher Created Materials, Inc.*
P.O. Box 1040
Huntington Beach, CA 92647
©1993 Teacher Created Materials, Inc.
Made in U.S.A.
ISBN 1-55734-278-4

Teacher Created Materials

# Table of Contents

# Introduction

*Food* is a captivating whole language, thematic unit. Its 80 exciting pages are filled with a wide variety of lesson ideas and reproducible pages designed for use with primary children. At its core are two high-quality children's literature selections, *Growing Vegetable Soup* and *The Milk Makers*. For these books, activities are included which set the stage for reading, encourage the enjoyment of the book, and extend the concepts gained. In addition, the theme is connected to the curriculum with activities in language arts (including daily writing suggestions), math, science, social studies, art, music, and life skills (cooking, physical education, career awareness, etc.). Many of these activities encourage cooperative learning. Suggestions and patterns for bulletin boards and unit management tools, and learning center ideas are additional time savers for the busy teacher. Furthermore, directions for student-created books and a culminating activity, which allow students to synthesize their knowledge in order to produce products that can be shared beyond the classroom, highlight this very complete teacher resource.

This thematic unit includes:

❏ **literature selections**—summaries of two children's books with related lessons (complete with reproducible pages) that cross the curriculum

❏ **poetry**—suggested selections and lessons enabling students to write and publish their own works

❏ **language experience and writing ideas**—suggestions as well as activities across the curriculum, including Big Books

❏ **bulletin board ideas**—suggestions and plans for student-created and/or interactive bulletin boards

❏ **homework suggestions**—extending the unit to the child's home

❏ **curriculum connections**—in language arts, math, science, art, music, and life skills such as cooking, and physical education

❏ **group projects**—to foster cooperative learning

❏ **a culminating activity**—which requires students to synthesize their learning to produce a product or engage in an activity that can be shared with others

❏ **a bibliography**—suggesting additional literature and nonfiction books on the theme

To keep this valuable resource intact so it can be used year after year, you may wish to punch holes in the pages and store them in a three-ring binder.

# Introduction *(cont.)*

## Why Whole Language?

A whole language approach involves children in using all modes of communication: reading, writing, listening, observing, illustrating, experiencing, and doing. Communication skills are interconnected and integrated into lessons that emphasize the whole of language rather than isolating its parts. The lessons revolve around selected literature. Reading is not taught as a separate subject from writing and spelling, for example. A child reads, writes (spelling appropriately for his/her level), speaks, listens, etc. in response to a literature experience introduced by the teacher. In this way, language skills grow naturally, stimulated by involvement and interest in the topic at hand.

## Why Thematic Planning?

One very useful tool for implementing an integrated whole language program is thematic planning. By choosing a theme with correlating literature selections for a unit of study, a teacher can plan activities throughout the day that lead to a cohesive, in-depth study of the topic. Students will be practicing and applying their skills in meaningful contexts. Consequently, they will tend to learn and retain more. Both teachers and students will be freed from a day that is broken into unrelated segments of isolated drill and practice.

## Why Cooperative Learning?

Besides academic skills and content, students need to learn social skills. No longer can this area of development be taken for granted. Students must learn to work cooperatively in groups in order to function well in modern society. Group activities should be a regular part of school life and teachers should consciously include social objectives as well as academic objectives in their planning. For example, a group working together to write a report may need to select a leader. The teacher should make clear to the students and monitor the qualities of good leader-follower group interaction just as he/she would state and monitor the academic goals of the project.

## Why Big Books?

An excellent cooperative, whole language activity is the production of Big Books. Groups of students, or the whole class, can apply their language skills, content knowledge, and creativity to produce a Big Book that can become a part of the classroom library to be read and reread. These books make excellent culminating projects for sharing beyond the classroom with parents, librarians, other classes, etc. Big Books can be produced in many ways, and this thematic unit book includes directions for at least one method you may choose.

## Why Journals?

Each day students should have the opportunity to write in a journal. They may respond to a book, write about a personal experience, or answer a general "question of the day" posed by the teacher. Students should be encouraged to refer to the posted vocabulary list to check their spelling. Teachers may read journals every day or choose to alternate days for boys and girls. This cumulative journal provides an excellent means of documenting writing progress.

4

# Growing Vegetable Soup

## by Lois Ehlert

### Summary

*Using colorful collages made from cut out pieces of paper, Lois Ehlert tells the story of a father and a child planting and tending a vegetable garden through the growing season. The author takes us through the "garden to table" process and leaves children with mouths watering for a taste of the "best soup ever." All the brilliantly colored items in the book are labeled for the reader.*

The outline below is a suggested plan for using the various activities in this unit. You may need to adapt this plan to meet the needs of your particular class.

## Sample Plan

### Day 1
- Introduce Book. (page 6)
- Set up activity centers. (pages 68-73)
- Prepare bulletin board. (page 76)
- Make Journal folders. (page 7, Enjoying the Book #5)
- Make Group Recipe. (page 6, Setting the Stage #2)
- Alphabetize foods. (page 9)
- Start Bean Sprouts. (page 49)
- Discuss food groups and balanced diets. (page 7, #2)
- Begin Food Journal. (page 7)
- Sing "Cook Has Put the Soup Pot On." (page 60)

### Day 2
- Start Food Journal. (page 7)
- Reread *Growing Vegetable Soup*. Create a class vegetable book. (page 6, Setting the Stage #3)
- Write a Garden Chant. (page 37)
- Do popcorn math on page 48 and sing a popcorn song on page 60.
- Begin "Garden of Growing Words." (page 6, Enjoying the Book #3)
- Homework: Garden, Orchard, Farm (page 6)

### Day 3
- Continue Food Journal. (page 7)
- Make vegetable soup. (page 6, Enjoying the Book #2)
- Begin Readers' Theater. (page 21)

- Find rhyming words. (page 42)
- Play some food games. (page 61)
- Locate stores on a map. (page 58)
- Try some "Pasta-bilities" activities. (pages 19-20)

### Day 4
- Continue Food Journal. (page 7)
- Read *On Market Street*. Do Market Street Math. (page 7, #8)
- Learn what a fruit is and what parts are edible. (page 8, #7,8)
- Identify shapes in a "Fruit Find." (pages 17-18)
- Draw Conclusions. (page 14)
- Play some food games. (page 61)

### Day 5
- Continue Food Journal. (page 7)
- Read and dramatize *The Little Red Hen*. (page 8, #13)
- Homework: Compare canned food labels. (page 7, #6)
- Sing "Oats, Peas, Beans and Barley Grow." (page 60)
- Practice ordinals with "A-Maze-ing Corn." (page 15)
- Write ABC Big Book. (page 40)
- Make Culminating Activity preparations. (page 67)

# Overview of Activities
## SETTING THE STAGE

1. List the color words red, green, orange, brown, yellow, and purple on the chalkboard. Ask students to suggest vegetable names to list under each color. This would be a good place to discuss what a vegetable is. (Botanical definition: a plant part, other than the fruit, that is edible.) If they name fruits (the reproductive part of a plant that contains the seed), make another heading for fruits and list all the fruits in one row. Announce that you are going to read a book to them about some colorful vegetables and that they will be learning about the many foods that we get from plants. As you read the book, ask students to watch for the listed vegetables and any new ones. Show the book. Ask students if it's possible to grow soup.

2. Pose the question: "How would you make vegetable soup?" Compose a group recipe on chart paper. Draw a large soup pot at the bottom and encourage each student to cut out a colorful vegetable to attach above the pot after listening to the story.

3. Read the story aloud, noting the labels and colorful collage art work. Create a class book titled "In Our Garden." Provide students with colorful construction paper, scissors, craft sticks, and markers. Have students contribute pages by cutting vegetables and other garden items out of the construction paper and gluing them onto 9" x 12" (23 cm x 30 cm) pieces of construction paper (similar to the pages in *Growing Vegetable Soup*). For identification, glue craft sticks with the vegetable names on them to the vegetables. Students may wish to create a similar class book about fruits.

4. Read the recipe for vegetable soup at the end of the story. Find the similarities and differences between the recipe written by the students and the recipe from the book. Use a Venn diagram to compare.

## ENJOYING THE BOOK

1. Classify foods by the part of the plant that is eaten. Then discuss where each of the vegetables from the book originate. Discuss examples of plant parts (fruit, roots, seeds, tuber, leaves, flowers) that are edible. Then have students fill in the chart on page 10.

2. Make vegetable soup in class. Ask students to bring ingredients and utensils to class. Use a simple, favorite recipe. It may be necessary to double or triple the recipe. This activity provides a good opportunity to practice math skills.

3. Make a "Garden of Growing Words." Label each of 26 library card pockets with a different letter of the alphabet. You may want the students to decorate the pocket with a food beginning with that alphabet letter. Then glue the 26 library card pockets onto large green poster board or tag board. As new words are encountered in the unit, students can write them on pre-cut slips of paper and "plant" them in the "Garden of Growing Words." Later on, the garden can be "replanted" using sorting by color, shape, etc.

4. Homework: Have students take home a paper divided into three sections: Garden, Orchard, Farm. Ask students to work with their families to see how many foods they can list in each section. Encourage them to bring in pictures of foods from magazines, newspapers, etc., to be used for displays and activities throughout the unit.

6

# Overview of Activities *(cont.)*

## ENJOYING THE BOOK *(cont.)*

5. Make Food Journal folders. Provide each student with a manila or construction paper folder to be used as a cover. Have students decorate the covers and attach several lined and unlined sheets to the folder. At the beginning of the unit, have students write and illustrate stories about their favorite foods, write sentences describing a particular food, etc. As you move further into the unit, have students use the Food Journal recording sheets on page 13 to name vegetables and fruits they have eaten each day. When discussing food products we get from animals, students can log meat and fish products. The information from the Food Journal may be used for classifying foods, studying the Food Pyramid (page 11), and learning how to balance a diet. Continue using the journal pages throughout the unit for relevant writing activities.

6. Homework: Have students compare two brands of canned fruits or vegetables from their kitchen shelf or the supermarket shelf. Encourage them to look for the following information on the product: weight, size of serving, fat, and sodium content, price, distributing state. Ask students to bring in can labels. Place them in a learning center for students to read and compare.

7. List all the people besides the gardener who are needed to bring food to our tables (truckers, farmers, veterinarians, bakers, botanists, meteorologists, ecologists, factory workers, beekeepers, etc.). Then ask students to "pick a career" to find out more about. You may want to invite several of the above to visit your classroom and discuss their jobs.

8. Bring a newspaper to class and note the grocery ads. Have students work in small groups to write and illustrate an advertisement to sell a chosen vegetable. Read *On Market Street* by Arnold Lobel (Greenwillow, 1981). In groups or individually, have students complete the "Market Street Math" problems on page 47.

## EXTENDING THE BOOK

1. Make a large "From Our Garden" bulletin board like the one shown on page 76. Plan the planting and labeling of your garden.

2. Stress the importance of a well balanced diet through adequate daily nutritional intake. In April of 1992, the U.S. Department of Agriculture replaced the "Food Wheel" with a pyramid graphic of dietary guidelines. A copy of the original pyramid is on page 11. Use this to discuss what foods comprise a daily balanced diet. Allow students to complete the food pyramid activity on page 12 and the hands-on activity on page 69 to create their own balanced meals.

3. Obtain literature on ketchup (see Resources, page 80). After reading the story of ketchup, make a bulletin board entitled "Ketchup on. . ." Have students write and/or illustrate all the foods they enjoy with ketchup. You may wish to include some more unusual ketchup combinations as well.

4. Take a closer look at breakfast cereals by making ingredient comparisons. Write a class letter to the Kellogg Company (see resources, page 80) for information.

5. Discuss with students how corn and other vegetables are prepared, canned, and distributed to markets. Ask students to follow the maze on page 15 to reinforce the corn canning process.

# Overview of Activities *(cont.)*
## EXTENDING THE BOOK *(cont.)*

6. Assign parts and prepare for the Readers' Theater play, "The Enormous Onion" (pages 21-22). Learn several of the songs from this unit (page 60) to share with a visiting class or parents as part of a culminating activity (see page 67).

7. Display several real seeds on a bulletin board with the caption, "Plant a Seed—Grow a Story." Discuss the parts of a fruit: seed or stone (endocarp), flesh (mesocarp), skin (exocarp). Try the following shoe box "fruit" activity with the class. Place two equal size shoe boxes (no lids) on a table. Obtain several empty matchboxes. Tape a 4" (10 cm) piece of yarn to each matchbox. Shred enough newspaper to fill the shoe boxes. Using these items, have students help you "assemble" a fruit so that the skin (box) houses the flesh (newspaper) and seeds (matchboxes). Use index cards for labeling fruit parts and place the shoe box "fruit" and labels at a center for students to use. Write interesting facts about fruit on index cards and add them to the center, along with pictures and books. Then, have students do the activity on page 16 and review the parts of the fruit and their functions.

8. Cut apart several kinds of fruits and observe the variety of seeds. If appropriate, discuss the nutritional value and taste appeal of various fruits. Prepare a fruit salad in class and enjoy the "fruits of your labor."

9. Read aloud *The Popcorn Book* by Tomie dePaola (Holiday House, 1978) to learn the origin and types of popcorn. Make and enjoy one of the recipes in the book. Try some popcorn math. Have students estimate how many unpopped kernels of popcorn there are in a jar. Provide pairs or teams of students with small bowls of colored popcorn kernels (available in most grocery stores). Have students sort kernels by color and create a color/number graph. Color in the graph with the matching color. Ask students to create their own math problems on page 48, using popped popcorn as manipulatives.

10. Have students write stories and poems using suggestions from the Poetry and Writing Activities section of this unit. Display student work on the bulletin board.

11. Bread, cereal, rice, and pasta comprise one part of the U.S Department of Agriculture's "Eating Right Pyramid" (see page 11). Discuss the nutritional benefits of these foods. Then have students try the pasta activities on pages 19-20.

12. Talk about and read the tongue twisters on page 43. Have students write their own food related tongue twisters on the lines provided. Cut out and display them in the classroom, or make a class Tasty Tongue Twisters class book.

13. Read and dramatize an available version of *The Little Red Hen*. Discuss the farm to table steps involved in making bread or cake. Talk about cooperation and sharing responsibilities. Make props and costumes and present the play to another class. Play the game on pages 44-45 stressing the blends and digraphs, and reinforcing the bread making process.

14. Plan a field trip to a local supermarket, cannery, or bakery. Send home field trip permission slips (page 77). Prepare students for each trip and provide follow-up activities for the class. Using the Supermarket Search (page 77), have students complete the chart of fruit and vegetable items. When they return to class, discuss and compare the students' Supermarket Search lists in terms of price, quality, packaging, and appeal.

8

**Name**_____

# Alphabet Soup

List 8 words from *Growing Vegetable Soup* that begin with the letters on the lines below.  Then write the words in ABC order on the carrots.

p _____     w _____

c _____     s _____

b _____     t _____

g _____     o _____

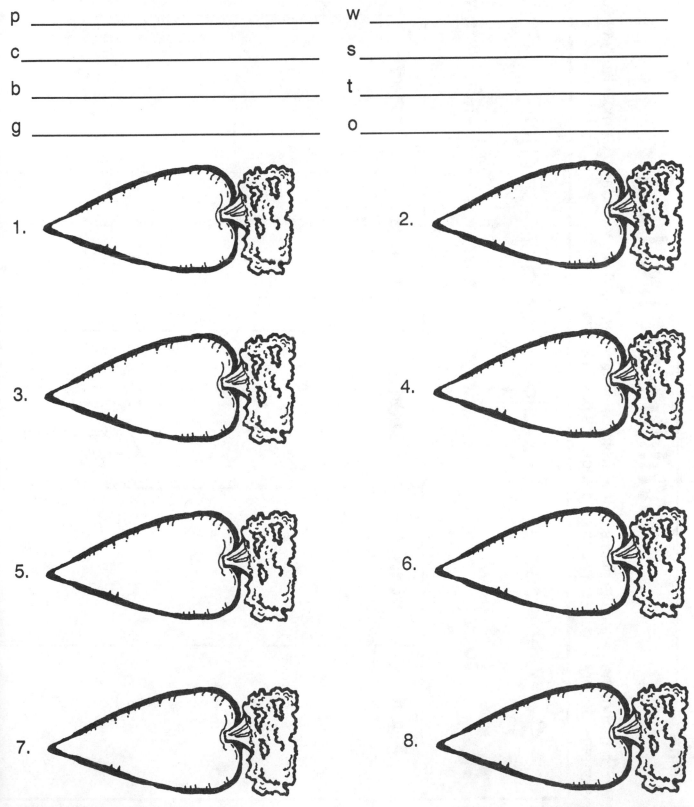

1.

2.

3.

4.

5.

6.

7.

8.

Name _____

# Which Part Do I Eat?

Which part of the vegetable plants below, from *Growing Vegetable Soup*, would you be most likely to eat? Write each vegetable under the correct heading to show the plant part that is eaten.

green beans    tomato    zucchini    pepper    potato

peas    onion    broccoli    corn    cabbage    carrots

| Fruit | Roots | Seeds | Tuber | Leaves | Flower |
|-------|-------|-------|-------|--------|--------|
|       |       |       |       |        |        |

10

Name_____

# Eat Right!

What kinds of foods do you eat each day?

Do you eat vegetables?_____     Do you eat fruit? _____

Do you eat yogurt? _____     Do you eat cereal? _____

Write the names of other foods you usually eat each day.

_____

_____

_____

_____

It is very important that we eat the right amounts and the right kinds of foods every day. That way we keep our bodies healthier and stronger. Study the chart below. It shows the kinds of foods you should eat each day and the number of servings you should have.

## Food Pyramid

**KEY**

● Fat (naturally occurring and added)

▼ Sugars (added)

These symbols show that fat and added sugars come mostly from fats, oils, and sweets, but can be part of or added to foods from the food groups as well.

A Guide to Daily Food Choices

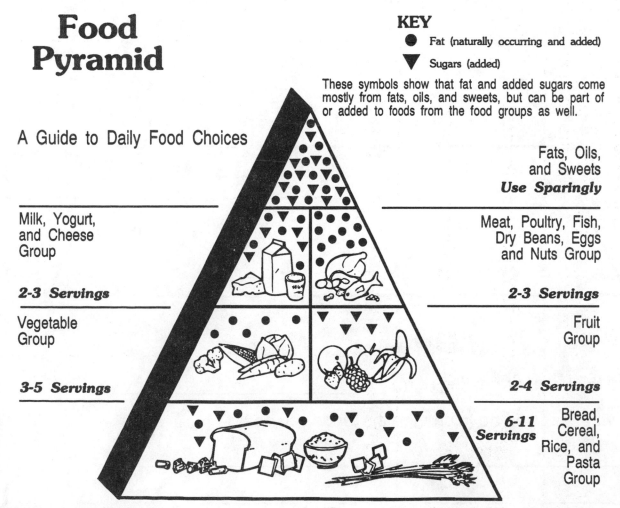

Fats, Oils, and Sweets
*Use Sparingly*

Milk, Yogurt, and Cheese Group

Meat, Poultry, Fish, Dry Beans, Eggs and Nuts Group

*2-3 Servings*

*2-3 Servings*

Vegetable Group

Fruit Group

*3-5 Servings*

*2-4 Servings*

*6-11 Servings*   Bread, Cereal, Rice, and Pasta Group

**Name** _____

# Eat Right! *(cont.)*

Fill in the chart on this page with the foods you ate in one day. Be sure to write the foods in the correct sections. Share your chart with your classmates.

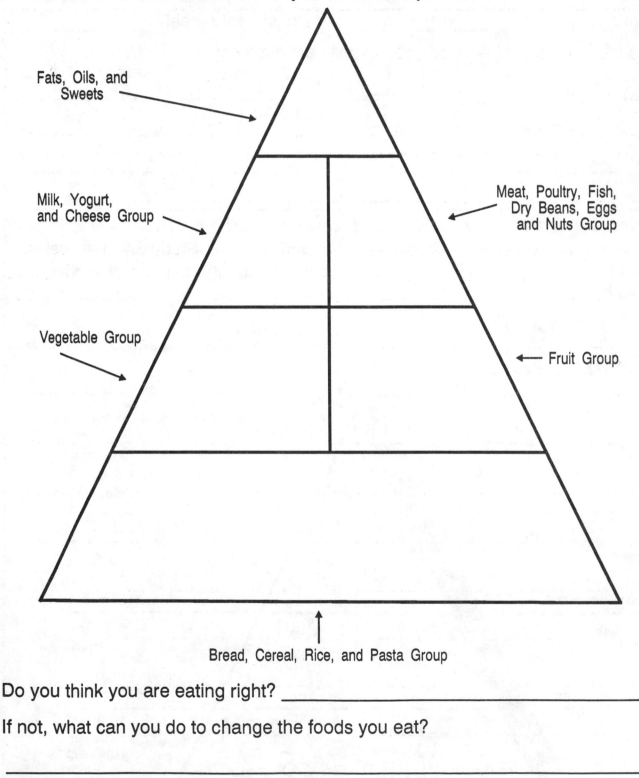

Do you think you are eating right? _____

If not, what can you do to change the foods you eat?

_____

_____

**Name**_____

# Food Journal

Think about some of the foods you ate yesterday. If one of the foods was a plant, write it in the plant column; if it came from an animal, write it in the animal column.

| Plant | Animal |
|-------|--------|
|       |        |
|       |        |
|       |        |
|       |        |
|       |        |
|       |        |
|       |        |
|       |        |
|       |        |
|       |        |
|       |        |

**Name** _____

# Drawing Conclusions

**Directions:** Read the story and decide where each picture should go. Cut out and glue the pictures on the correct boxes in the story. Then, read and answer the questions which follow the story.

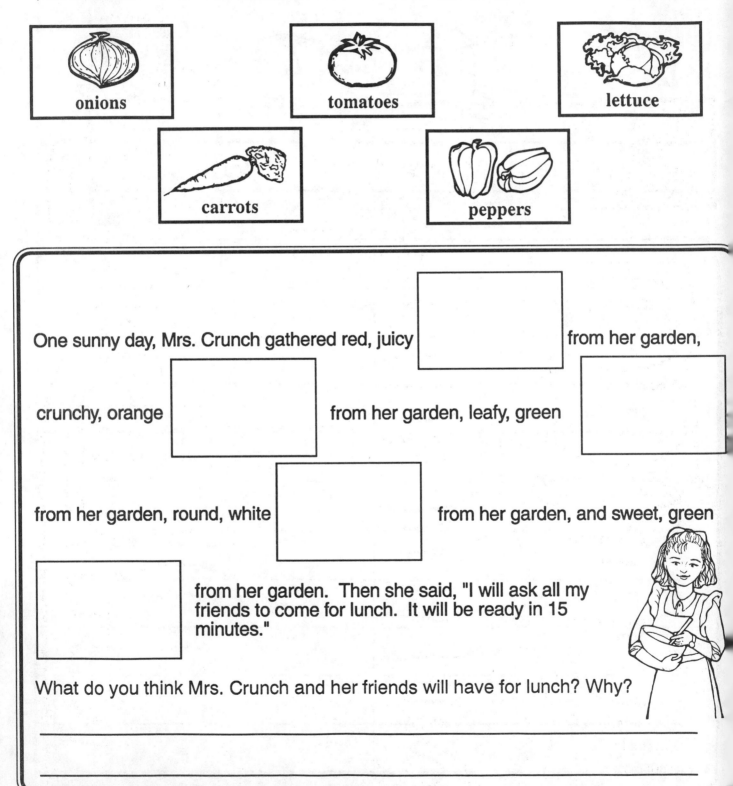

One sunny day, Mrs. Crunch gathered red, juicy [ ] from her garden,

crunchy, orange [ ] from her garden, leafy, green [ ]

from her garden, round, white [ ] from her garden, and sweet, green

[ ] from her garden.  Then she said, "I will ask all my friends to come for lunch.  It will be ready in 15 minutes."

What do you think Mrs. Crunch and her friends will have for lunch? Why?

_____

_____

Name_____

*Growing Vegetable Soup*

# A-Maze-ing Corn

**Directions**: Follow the maze from the can of corn to your house. With a pencil or your finger, trace the path. As you come to a can, write the correct ordinal word on the line. The words are listed below.

1. first
2. second
3. third
4. fourth
5. fifth
6. sixth
7. seventh
8. eighth

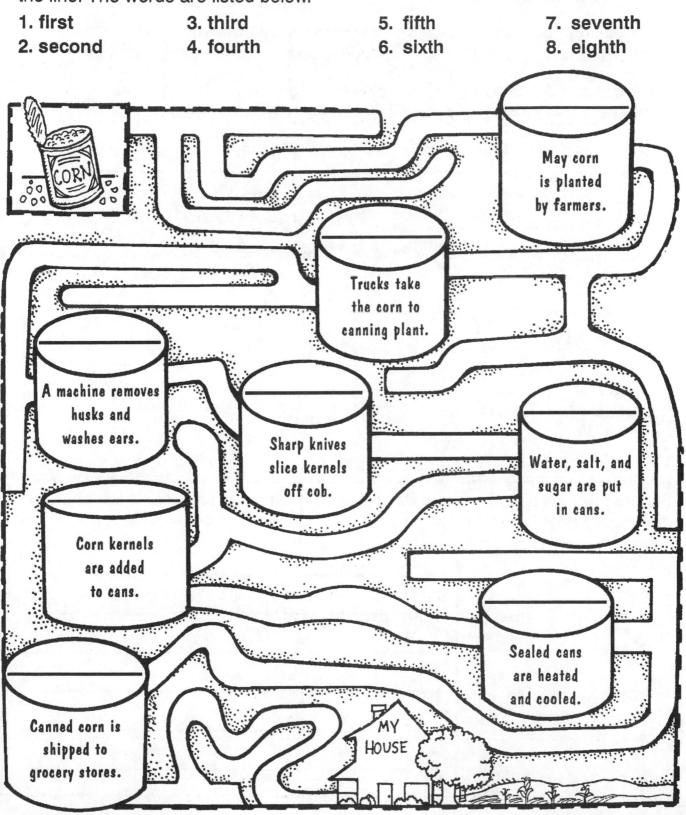

**Name** _____

# What's A Fruit?

Do you like to eat fruit? _____

What is your favorite kind of fruit? _____

Besides tasting good, fruits help us to stay healthy by giving us the important nutrients we need. You should eat from two to four servings of fruit each day.

A fruit is the part of the plant that contains the seed. The seeds of a plant grow into a new plant. The fruit part of a plant is like a house for seeds.

Here is the inside of a fruit you might like to eat—the peach. It has three parts.

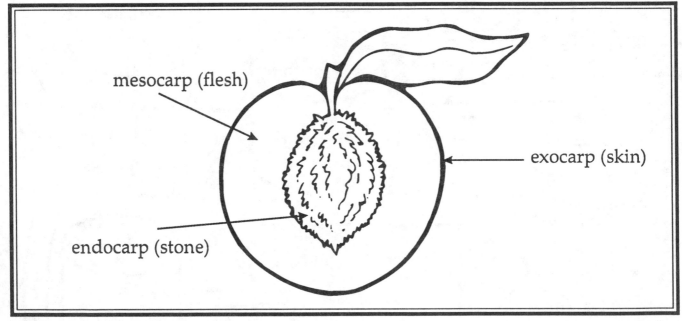

mesocarp (flesh)

exocarp (skin)

endocarp (stone)

In the box, draw a picture of your favorite fruit. Then write a few sentences about it on the lines below.

**Name**_____

# Fruit Find

Not all fruits grow on trees. Bananas grow on a tree-like plant. Grapes grow on a vine. Look at the fruits on this page. Decide whether they grow on a tree or on the ground. Cut out the pictures along the dashed lines and glue them on or under the tree on page 18. Make a list of other fruits on the back of page 18.

**Name** _____

# Fruit Find *(cont.)*

See page 17 for directions.

# Pasta-bilities

## Class Activities

1. Write a class letter to Martha Gooch products at the following address:

   **Gooch Foods, Inc.**
   **Lincoln, Nebraska  68501-0808**

   Ask to borrow any educational materials available.

2. Paint some macaroni with markers or paints. Or, soak them in water and food coloring (to desired color) and let dry. String the macaroni on string or yarn to make jewelry. Or, prepare several colors of dyed macaroni and create macaroni mosaics. Have students title their creations and display them.

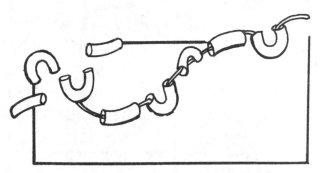

3. Bring several varieties of pasta to school. Let the students choose two or three to incorporate into a picture. (The pasta bows make nice butterfly shapes and can be added to a garden scene; pasta shells can be glued onto an ocean scene; pasta wheels could be fastened to an illustrated truck or car.)

4. Duplicate the twelve cards on the next page for the following Spaghetti Stretch activity. On the back of each of the twelve cards, write a different month of the year. This will determine the order in which the cards are read. Laminate the page for durability and cut out the cards. Pass the cards out randomly to students in different areas of the room.  Place an unwrapped skein of yellow yarn (the spaghetti) in a big bowl. Pull out the end of the yarn and pass it to the student holding the January card. He/she reads the card orally and passes the end of the spaghetti to the person holding the February card while still holding the "spaghetti" yarn. The fun continues as each month's card is read. Soon there will be a roomful of "spaghetti." Collect the cards and repeat the process with a different group of students.

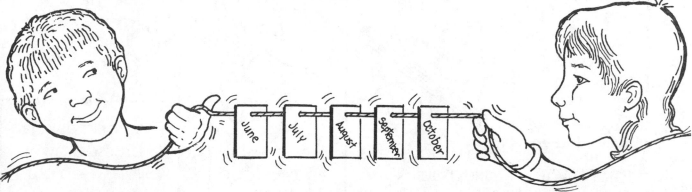

5. Read *Strega Nona*, a tale retold and illustrated by Tomie dePaola (Simon & Schuster, 1975).

# Pasta-bilities *(cont.)*

## Spaghetti Stretch

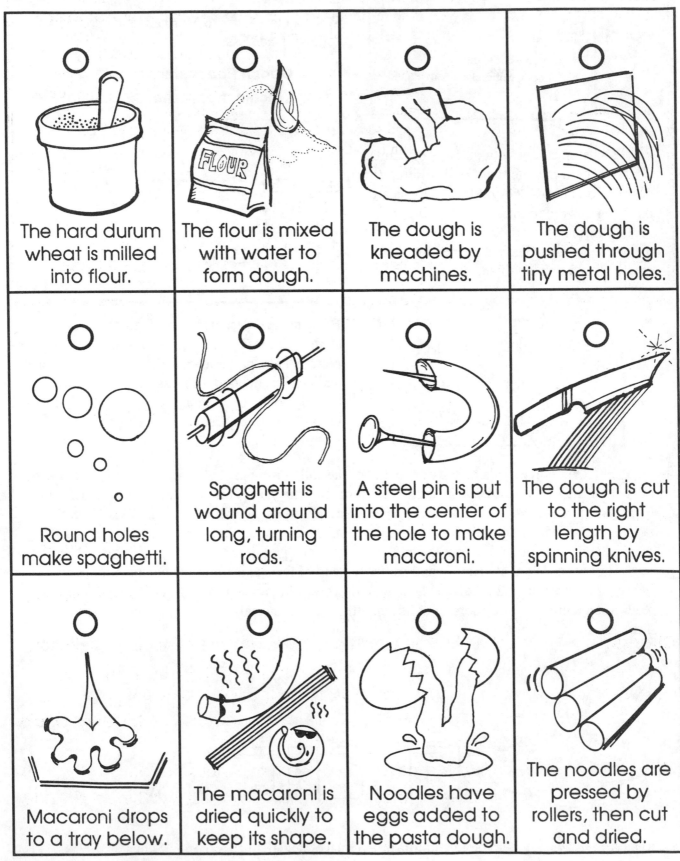

The hard durum wheat is milled into flour.

The flour is mixed with water to form dough.

The dough is kneaded by machines.

The dough is pushed through tiny metal holes.

Round holes make spaghetti.

Spaghetti is wound around long, turning rods.

A steel pin is put into the center of the hole to make macaroni.

The dough is cut to the right length by spinning knives.

Macaroni drops to a tray below.

The macaroni is dried quickly to keep its shape.

Noodles have eggs added to the pasta dough.

The noodles are pressed by rollers, then cut and dried.

# Readers' Theater

Readers' Theater is an exciting and relatively easy method of providing students with the opportunity to perform a mini-play with the minimal use (or absence) of props, sets, elaborate costumes, or memorization. Students read the dialogue of a character in a book or prepared script, or they can become the narrators to provide background information, or chorus, by reading the remaining words. The dialogue, narration, or chorus may be read verbatim as the author has written it, or an elaboration may be written by the performing students. Sound effects and dramatic voices can make these much like radio plays. For the following play, you may wish to prepare a simple background and some easy-to-make costumes described below.

**Preparation:** Paint a garden background. If possible, scatter some corn stalks and artificial or real plants or flowers around the garden. Make a large onion shape and attach it to the back of a small chair. As indicated in the script, have the children just pretend to pull until the worm comes to help; then pull the onion off the chair. The children could make headbands with the names of their vegetables on the front, or they could make paper grocery bag vests (have them put a large picture of their vegetable on the back and two smaller ones on the front). The gardener will need to make his/her tools and gloves on this headband or vest. The worm art could go all the way around the vest.

## The Enormous Onion

**Characters:**

| | | |
|---|---|---|
| Gardener | Cabbage | Zucchini |
| Tomato | Green Bean | Peas ( 2 or 3) |
| Worm | Corn | Chorus (remaining students) |
| Carrot | Green Pepper | Broccoli |
| Potatoes (2 or 3) | | |

**Gardener:** One day I planted an onion in my garden.

**Chorus:** And it grew and it grew and it grew!

**Gardener:** When I tried to pull it up to make vegetable soup, the onion was enormous. *(Gardener tugs at onion.)*

*As each character enters to help the gardener, he or she pulls and tugs, trying to lift it out of the ground.*

**Chorus:** He pulled and he pulled and he pulled, but the onion would not budge!

**Gardener:** Broccoli! Please, come and help me pull this onion!

**Chorus:** They pulled and they pulled and they pulled, but the onion would not budge!

**Broccoli:** Green Bean! Please, come and help us pull this onion!

**Chorus:** They pulled and they pulled and they pulled, but the onion would not budge!

**Green Bean:** Corn! Please, come and help us pull this onion!

# Readers' Theater *(cont.)*

### The Enormous Onion *(cont.)*

**Chorus:** They pulled and they pulled and they pulled, but the onion would not budge!

**Corn:** Carrot! Please, come and help us pull the onion!

**Chorus:** They pulled and they pulled and they pulled, but the onion would not budge!

**Carrot:** Cabbage! Please, come and help us pull this onion!

**Chorus:** They pulled and they pulled and they pulled, but the onion would not budge!

**Cabbage:** Tomato! Please, come and help us pull this onion!

**Chorus:** They pulled and they pulled and they pulled, but the onion would not budge!

**Tomato:** Peas! Please, come and help us pull this onion!

**Chorus:** They pulled and they pulled and they pulled, but the onion would not budge!

**Peas:** Potatoes! Please, come and help us pull this onion!

**Chorus:** They pulled and they pulled and they pulled, but the onion would not budge!

**Potatoes:** Green Pepper! Please, come and help us pull this onion!

**Chorus:** They pulled and they pulled and they pulled, but the onion would not budge!

**Green Pepper:** Zucchini! Please, come and help us pull this onion!

**Chorus:** They pulled and they pulled and they pulled, but the onion would not budge!

**Zucchini:** Worm! Here is your chance to be helpful in the garden. Please, come and help us pull this onion!

**Gardener:** Boo! Hoo!

**Broccoli:** Sniff! Sniff!

**Green Bean:** Waa! Waa!

**Corn:** Sob! Sob! *(etc., until everyone has cried!)*

**Everyone:** *(shaking their heads)* That onion will never be part of our soup! It is too hard to pull out of the ground.

**Worm:** No it isn't! If we all tug our hardest, we can do it!

**Chorus:** Everyone looked at the worm. If he can do it, they thought, so can we! And they pulled and pulled and pulled. Suddenly, the onion was yanked out...and all the vegetables fell to the ground in a heap! What a delicious soup they will make after all!

22

# The Milk Makers

## by Gail Gibbons

### Summary

The Milk Makers *gives a colorful and concise explanation of how cows are able to produce milk, what happens to the milk after it leaves the farm, and the many products we enjoy that started out as milk. It is a very informative book for young readers on dairy cows and the milk production process. Illustrations are clearly labeled. Children will come away with a better understanding of the processing of milk after it is transported to the dairy.* The Milk Makers *was named an American Library Association Notable Book and a Reading Rainbow feature selection.*

The outline below is a suggested plan for using the various activities in this unit. You may need to adapt this plan to meet the needs of your class.

## Sample Plan

### Day 1

- Introduce and read *The Milk Makers*. (page 24, Setting the Stage #1,2)
- Continue Food Journals. (page 7, Enjoying the Book #5)
- Sequence milk process from farm to table. (pages 26-27)
- Examine drops of milk. (page 49)
- Sing "Old McDonald Had a Cow." (page 60)
- Measure liquids and find equivalent amounts. (page 24, Enjoying the Book #2)

### Day 2

- Continue Food Journals. (page 7)
- Learn about other milk makers. Assemble mini-book. (page 24, Enjoying the Book #4)
- Discuss healthy eating habits and nutrients. (page 56)
- Assemble and write stories for Lift and Look Books. (page 41)
- Do Dairy Fat Test. (page 49)
- Make Magic Cow Floats. (page 65)

### Day 3

- Continue Food Journals. (page 7)
- Locate some U.S. food producing states. (page 59)
- Practice telling time. (page 30)

- Learn about curds and whey. (page 25, #3)
- Make desk top cow and write cow stories. (page 24)
- Learn how cheese is made. (page 31)

### Day 4

- Continue Food Journals. (page 7)
- Explore foods through the five senses. (page 53)
- Make cow bookmarks. (page 64)
- Learn how honey comes to the table. Write a Busy Bee Story. (page 25, #2)
- Discover how chocolate is made. (page 25, #1)
- Assemble file folder accordion books. (page 41)

### Day 5

- Continue Food Journal. (page 7)
- Make butter. (page 65)
- Play From Green Grass to White Milk game. (pages 32-36)
- Discuss the meat group and make Mrs. Pig Wheel. (page 25, #7)
- Solve A-Fishing We Will Go problems. (page 46)
- Make Pencil Pals. (page 64)

# Overview of Activities

## SETTING THE STAGE

1. Remind students that all our food comes from plants or animals. Make a list on the chalkboard of animals that supply us with food. Have students use the Food Journal (page 13) to keep a daily log of meat or fish products they eat. Ask if any of the listed animals are milk makers. Food items from their journal can be discussed in terms of the Food Pyramid and daily nutritional needs.

2. Read *The Milk Makers* to the class. There is so much information in Gail Gibbons' book that you may want to make a black and white gallon jug-shaped Big Book entitled "Cool Facts About Milk" or "Udderly Interesting Facts." Discuss fiction and nonfiction.

3. Put a large sheet of black paper with lots of Holstein-shaped white spots on it. Label it "Dairy Dictionary." As new words such as pasteurization and homogenization are encountered in the unit, number them and put them on the white spots.

## ENJOYING THE BOOK

1. Place about 12 food pictures along the chalkboard ledge or on a wall display. Number them and ask students to choose one to describe in writing without using the name of the food or its number. These could be written in the Food Journal. Ask students to read their descriptions aloud to see if classmates can guess the right picture.

2. Provide measuring cups and pint, quart, and gallon size containers in a learning center (see page 68). Use metric measuring containers in addition to, or to replace these, if desired. Have children experiment with liquids to see how many pints equal a quart, how many milliliters equal a liter, etc. Make a class chart of equivalent measures using the information from students' discoveries.

3. Reinforce the milk making process by having students play the game on pages 32-36.

4. Discuss with students the fact that the cow is a mammal and that mammals are milk makers. Run copies of pages 28-29 back to back. Trim the excess edge of the paper by cutting around the outer box. Cut the paper in half along the dashed line. Place the top half of the page (8,1) over the bottom half (6,3). Fold in half along the book spine and staple. Read and illustrate the Mini-Book.

5. Practice telling time with the Milking Time story on page 30.

6. Reproduce the cow and barn patterns on page 63 using index paper or tag board (or glue copies to heavy paper). Have students assemble the Mooo-ving Cow. Ask students to recall all the information they have learned about cows and dairy farms. List student responses on a chart or chalkboard. Students can use these ideas for writing stories. Or, provide story starter sentences based on the information suggested by the students.

7. Reproduce the cow pattern on page 62 using index paper or tag board. Have students cut out, assemble, and color the Desk Top Story Starter and write a story about "A Day in the Life of a Cow."

24

# Overview of Activities *(cont.)*

## EXTENDING THE BOOK

1. Chocolate is one of the many food products that uses milk as an ingredient. Ask students if they know where chocolate comes from. Give each student a piece of fingerpainting paper and squirt some instant chocolate pudding (use a ketchup or syrup bottle) in the middle of it. Discuss the taste and texture of the pudding and talk about the various chocolate products children may enjoy. Use page 50 to learn about the origin of chocolate. Have students write a chocolate story in their Food Journals. Or, cut large chocolate kiss shapes from aluminum foil and attach students' stories to them for a wall or bulletin board display. Share real chocolate kisses with the class. Discuss with students the importance of limiting sweets (see Food Pyramid).

2. Read aloud *From Blossom to Honey* by Ali Mitgutsch (Carolrhoda, 1981). If possible, invite a local beekeeper to class. Perhaps he/she can bring protective clothing and a hive. Make honey butter by adding 3 tablespoons (45 mL) of honey to 1 cup (250 mL) of softened butter. The honey butter could be served on biscuits, soda crackers, or graham crackers. Have students sequence The Busy Bee story on pages 54-55. Write a Honey of a Story class book using suggestions on page 54. Talk about the plants which provide sweeteners for our food.

3. Read aloud the nursery rhyme, "Little Miss Muffet." Discuss the terms curds and whey. (Curd is the coagulated part of soured milk. The watery part that separates from the curd is the whey.) Tell students that the curds and whey in "Little Miss Muffet" are similar to cottage cheese. The recipe on page 65 approximates the cheese making process. Have students complete the Cheese Please activity on page 31.

4. The origin of cottage cheese is unknown, but you might want to have a cheese tasting party using some of the following cheeses: cheddar—England; Colby—United States; Edam—Holland; Gouda—Holland; Swiss—Switzerland; Mozzarella—Italy; Blue—France; Parmesan—Italy; Muenster—Germany; Ricotta—Italy. Locate the origins of each of the cheeses on a world map.

5. Plan a field trip to a creamery or dairy farm, if possible. Using the farm stationery on page 78, have students write a letter to a friend telling about the field trip.

6. Talk about the foods we get from the fish group. Find the recommended daily servings of fish on the Food Pyramid (page 11). Ask students to name their favorite fish or sea food. Read the fish poem on page 57 and locate the oceans of the world in which fish may be found. Prepare appropriate level math problems on the fish shapes on page 46. Ask students to solve the problems and have them color all fish with answers greater than a given number.

7. Using Food Journal lists or a class food chart, review which foods belong to the meat group and the recommended daily servings of meat on the Food Pyramid. Reproduce pages 51 and 52 on index paper and have students assemble the Thank You Mrs. Pig wheel. Discuss the food products we get from pigs.

8. Review the plant and animal origins of some of the foods we eat using the students' Food Journals. On the map on page 59, identify some of the food producing states in the United States. Do some research to find the areas where most of the cattle ranches and pig farms are located. Add this information to the map.

9. Distribute copies of page 56 and discuss what nutrients are and how they help us to maintain good health.

# From Farm to Table

**Directions:** Number the pictures in the correct order so that they tell the story of milk. Put the number in the small box inside each picture. Have your teacher check your answers. Then, cut out the pictures and glue them on top of the matching number on the barn on page 27. Color the barn and tell someone "The Story of Milk."

  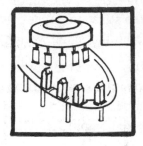

26

Name _____

# From Farm to Table *(cont.)*

See page 26 for directions.

# Mini-Book

See page 24 for directions.

The cow is a milk maker. These animals are also milk making mammals. (List five mammals.)

_____

_____

_____

_____

_____

8

# Milk Making Mammals

**This mini-book belongs to**

_____

1

Some mammals live in a tree. Draw and label a mammal that lives in a tree.

6

All mammals have hair or fur on their bodies. Color the mammal on this page. Write its name on the line.

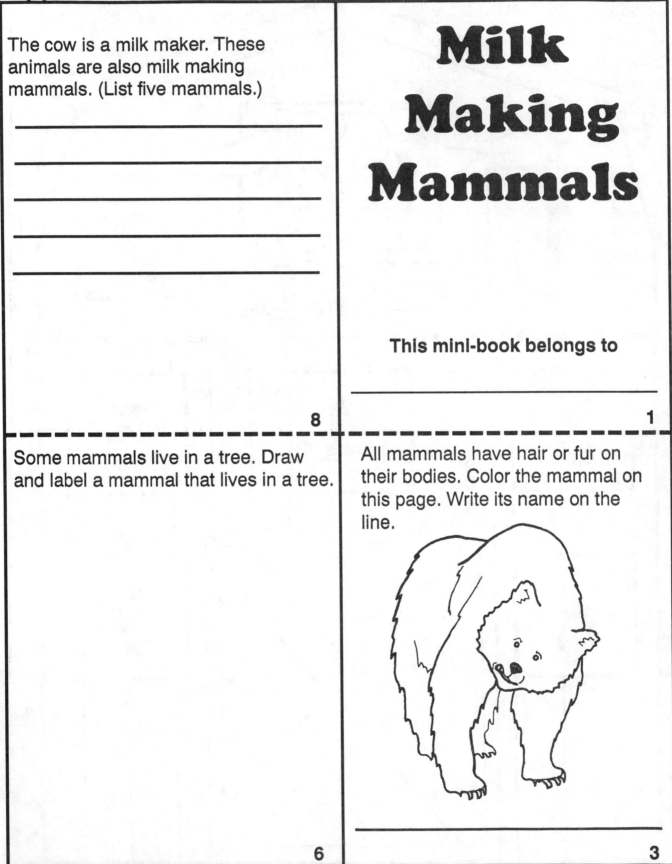

_____

3

28

# Mini-Book *(cont.)*

See page 24 for directions.

All mammals feed their babies milk. All mammals have warm blood. Color this mammal and her baby. Write the name of the mammal on the line.

_____

2

Some mammals are tame. Draw and label a tame mammal.

7

Some mammals live on a farm. Draw and label a farm mammal.

4

Some mammals live in the sea. Draw and label a sea mammal.

5

**Name** _____

# Milking Time

**Directions**: Read the sentences in each box below. They tell a story about the journey of milk from farm to dairy to store. Draw clock hands on the clocks to show the times listed in each box.

**4:00 A.M.**
The farmer begins his day.

**5:00 A.M.**
The cows are taken to the barn.

**6:30 A.M.**
The dairy tank truck takes the milk to the dairy.

**7:00 A.M.**
The milk goes through the clarifier.

**7:15 A.M.**
Some of the milk is separated from the cream.

**7:25 A.M.**
The milk is pasteurized to "kill" the bacteria.

**8:00 A.M.**
The milk is homogenized to break up the fat.

**8:45 A.M.**
Milk is put into cartons and taken to the store.

**5:05 P.M.**
The milking begins again!

Name_____

# Cheese Please!

**Directions:** Fill in the blanks below to complete the story of cheese making. You will find the words you need on the pieces of cheese at the bottom of the page. Share the story in class or at home.

Cheese making begins with **p**_____milk.

Then **r**_____is added to the milk. The lumps that form are

called **c**_____. The liquid that is left is called **w**_____.

First, the milk must be **h**_____. Large **k**_____ cut

the curd into small pieces. Some **s**_____is added to the curds. The

curds are pressed into a solid block of **c**_____.

pasteurized

knives

whey

rennet

cheese

heated

salt

curds

# From Green Grass to White Milk

**Materials**: scissors; pages 33-36 (one set for each group) reproduced on index paper; brads (one per group); glue or tape

**Teacher Directions:** For each group of 2 or 3 students attach pages 33 and 34 with tape or glue to form a game board. You may want to laminate the game board, spinner, markers, and cards for durability. Cut out the game cards and distribute a set to each group. Groups should place them face down on a playing surface. Have each group cut out and assemble the spinner (students may need help with this). Color and cut out the markers below and place them on the starting line. Establish which player in each group will go first by the highest spin on the spinner. Provide each team with a copy of the answer key card below.

**Spinner:** Cut out the spinner and arrow. Punch a hole in the center of the spinner and arrow. Attach the arrow to the spinner with a brad. If the arrow does not spin freely, loosen the brad a little.

**Student Directions:** Turn a game card over. Read it and decide which word (from the game board cartons) completes the sentence. If you are correct, spin the spinner and move your marker ahead the same number of spaces as shown by your spin of the spinner. If you are incorrect, you lose a turn. The next player takes a turn. The first player to reach the end space is the winner.

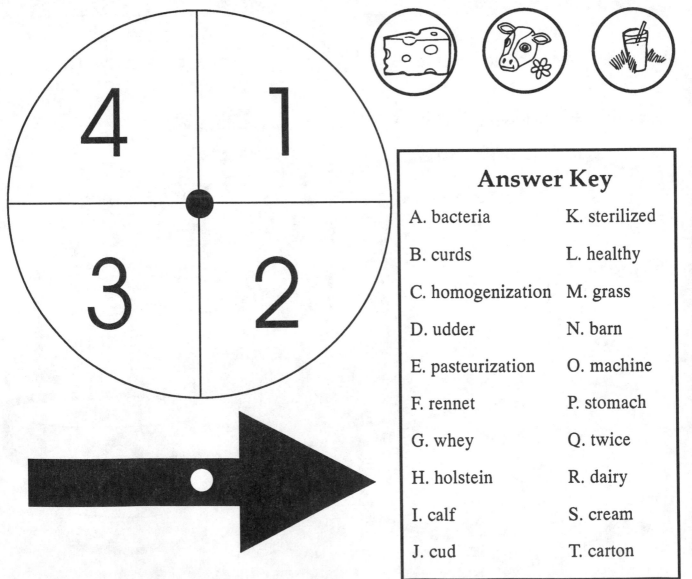

## Answer Key

| | |
|---|---|
| A. bacteria | K. sterilized |
| B. curds | L. healthy |
| C. homogenization | M. grass |
| D. udder | N. barn |
| E. pasteurization | O. machine |
| F. rennet | P. stomach |
| G. whey | Q. twice |
| H. holstein | R. dairy |
| I. calf | S. cream |
| J. cud | T. carton |

# From Green Grass

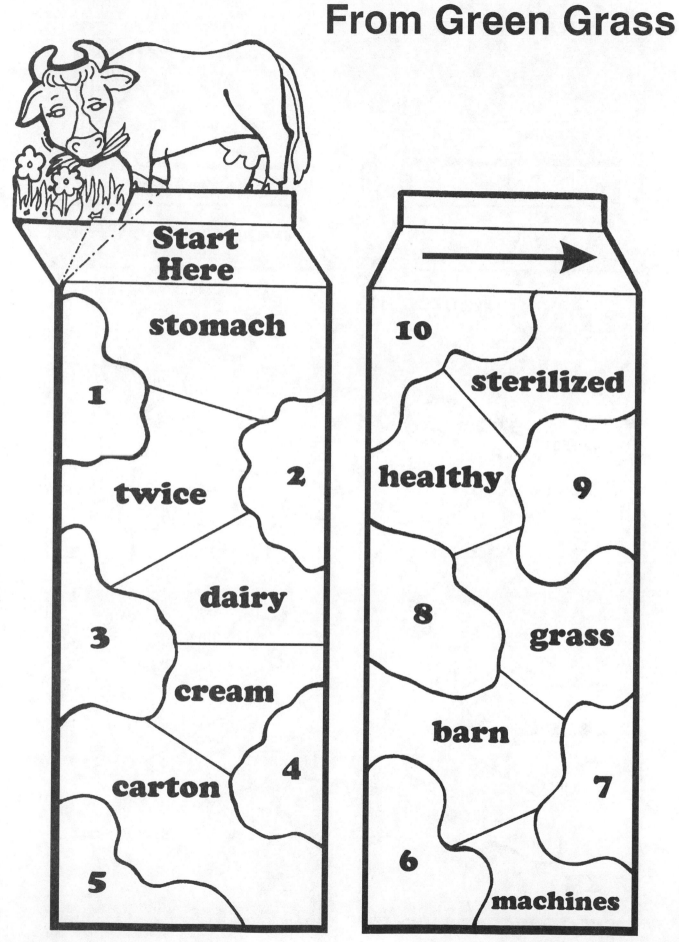

Start
Here

stomach

1

twice

2

dairy

3

cream

carton

4

5

10

sterilized

healthy

9

8

grass

barn

7

6

machines

# to White Milk *(cont.)*

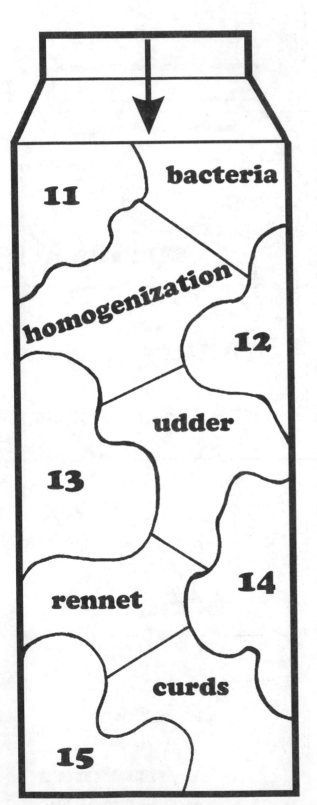

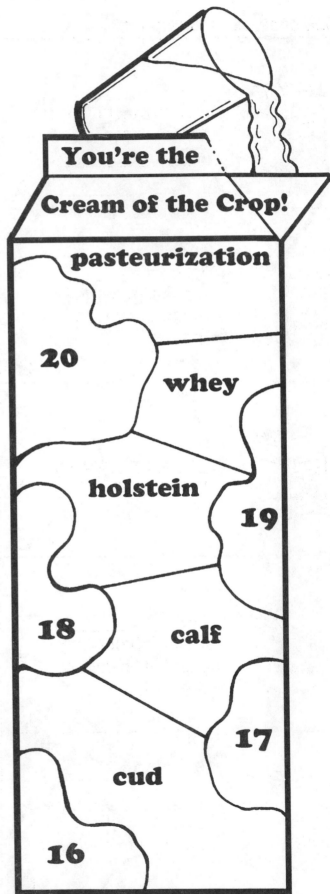

34

# Game Cards

See page 32 for directions.

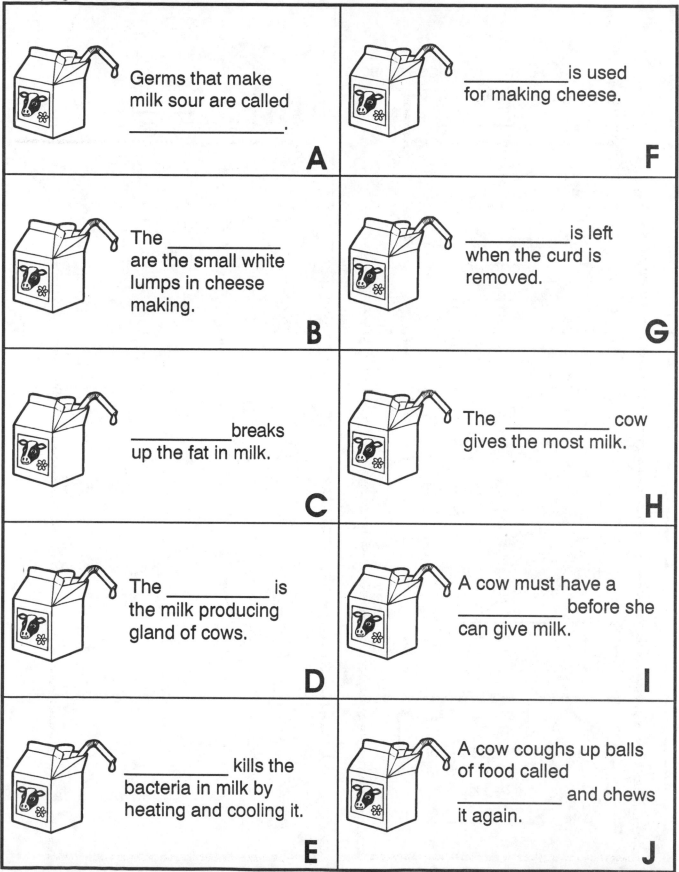

Germs that make milk sour are called _____.

**A**

_____ is used for making cheese.

**F**

The _____ are the small white lumps in cheese making.

**B**

_____ is left when the curd is removed.

**G**

_____ breaks up the fat in milk.

**C**

The _____ cow gives the most milk.

**H**

The _____ is the milk producing gland of cows.

**D**

A cow must have a _____ before she can give milk.

**I**

_____ kills the bacteria in milk by heating and cooling it.

**E**

A cow coughs up balls of food called _____ and chews it again.

**J**

# Game Cards *(cont.)*

See page 32 for directions.

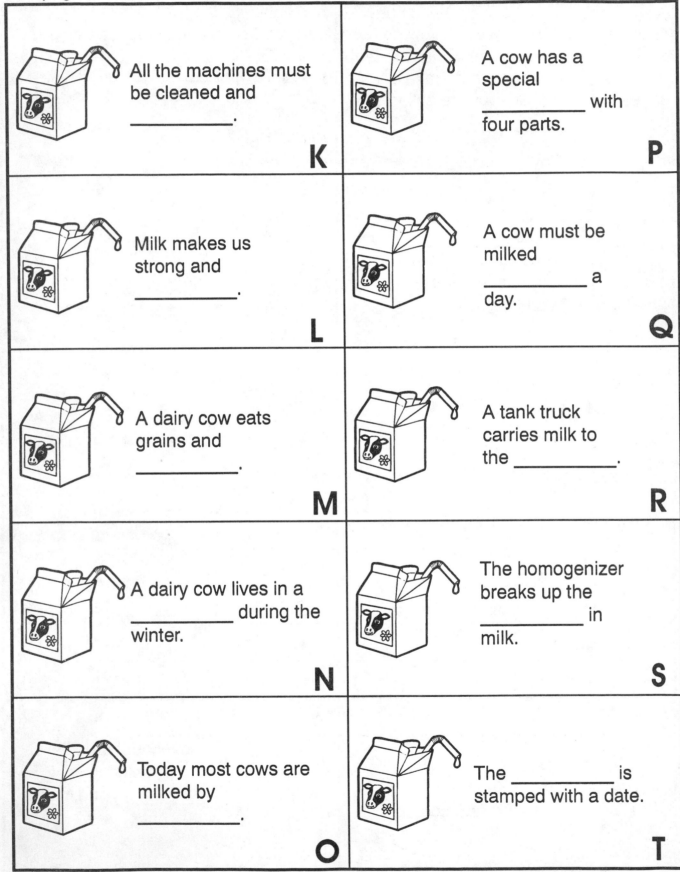

All the machines must be cleaned and _____.

**K**

A cow has a special _____ with four parts.

**P**

Milk makes us strong and _____.

**L**

A cow must be milked _____ a day.

**Q**

A dairy cow eats grains and _____.

**M**

A tank truck carries milk to the _____.

**R**

A dairy cow lives in a _____ during the winter.

**N**

The homogenizer breaks up the _____ in milk.

**S**

Today most cows are milked by _____.

**O**

The _____ is stamped with a date.

**T**

36

# Let's Write a Garden Chant!

**Directions:**   Read the garden chant below. Replace the parts that tell about the green bean with one of the following foods: pea pod; tomato; squash; pumpkin; pepper; apple; strawberry. Color the plant border. Share your garden chant with the class. Then, put your poem into your Food Journal or cut it out and display it in the classroom.

*In a green, green garden*
*There was a green, green plant.*
*On that green, green plant*
*There was a white, white flower.*
*From that white, white flower*
*There grew a green, green bean.*
*Green Beans - YUM!*

### In a Green, Green Garden

_____

_____

_____

_____

_____

_____

_____

_____

_____

*by*_____

# Seed Package Stories

**Directions:** Cut out the seed package below. Fold Section B behind Section A along the fold line. Fold flaps 1 and 2 back and glue them to Section B. Leave the top flap open. On a separate piece of paper, write a story or poem, or tell some interesting facts you know about a plant that grows from a seed. On the cover of the seed package (Section A) write a title and draw a picture of the seed plant. Fold your story and slip it into the seed package. Share your story with the class.

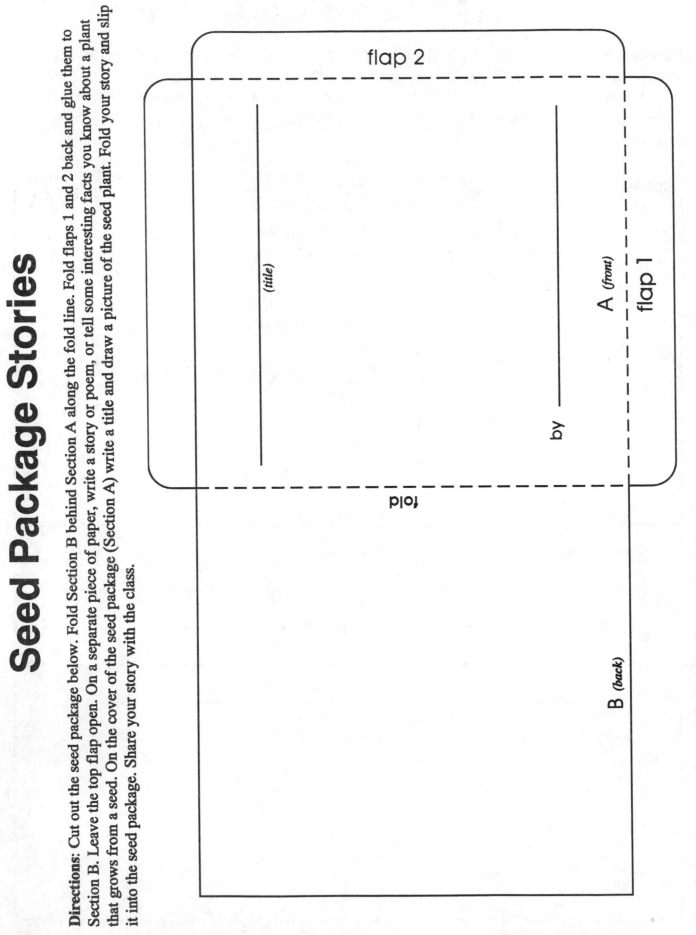

flap 2

(title)

A *(front)*

by

flap 1

fold

B *(back)*

# My Seed Book

**Directions**: Cut the seed book along the dashed lines. Fold down along the solid line, so that pages 2 and 3 are behind pages 1 and 4. Fold on the line between pages 1 and 4 to make a book. Tape or glue some real seeds (bean, corn, pea, cucumber, etc.) to page 1 of the seed book. Read and complete the sentences in the seed book. Draw pictures to go with the sentences.

My _____ seeds
need rain.

3

My _____ seeds
need sunshine.

2

Soon my _____ seeds will
look like this.

4

*My Seed Book*

by _____

These are _____ seeds.
I will plant them in my garden.

1

# ABC Big Book

Big Books can be created by students in groups, individually, or as a class. They may contain a predetermined text, or students may wish to provide both text and illustrations.

**Teacher Preparation:** Provide each student with a 12" x 18" (30 cm x 46 cm) piece of construction paper, index paper, or tag board. Have students write the ABC's down the right side of their Big Book pages, as shown. Assign each student (or have students choose) a letter of the alphabet. Have students highlight on their papers the letter of the alphabet for which they will be responsible.

Before starting your Big Book, you may want to read aloud *Eating the Alphabet: Fruits & Vegetables from A to Z* by Lois Ehlert (HBJ, 1989).

**Directions:** Using the ABC paper, ask each student to write a four line description or poem of a vegetable or fruit that begins with his or her assigned letter. Add illustrations to the page. Model the assignment and brainstorm suggestions using some of the following examples:

*A is for apples.*

*An apple is a fruit.*

*Apples grow on trees.*

*We use apples to make _____.*

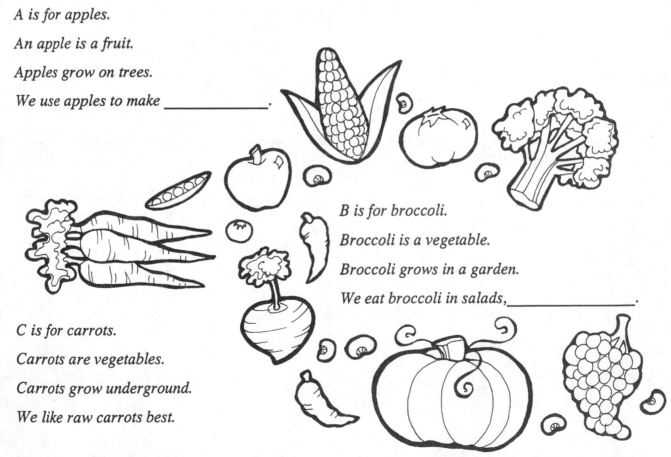

*B is for broccoli.*

*Broccoli is a vegetable.*

*Broccoli grows in a garden.*

*We eat broccoli in salads,_____.*

*C is for carrots.*

*Carrots are vegetables.*

*Carrots grow underground.*

*We like raw carrots best.*

**Assembling the Big Book:** When each student has completed and illustrated his/her alphabet page, bind the student pages on the sides or top with rings, holes and yarn, or a binding machine. The cover can be made from construction paper, index, or tag board. Laminate the cover for durability. Place the Big Book at a center for all to share.

# More Book Making Ideas

## Lift and Look Books

Although the directions for making the following Lift and Look Book are designed to show the four seasons on a dairy farm, they can be used to create books which will enhance other writing experiences.

**Directions**: Follow these steps to create a Lift and Look Book.

1. Fold a large sheet of construction paper, index paper, or tag board in half lengthwise.
2. Fold the paper into four sections, as shown.
3. Open the sheet of paper and cut along one side of the small folds to the center fold.
4. Write Summer, Winter, Spring, and Fall on the flaps. Under the appropriate flaps, illustrate the seasons on the dairy farm and add text, if desired.

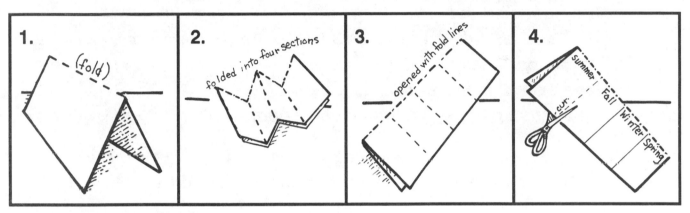

## File Folder Accordion Books

Accordion books can be created by individual students, in small groups, or as a class project. Life cycles, poetry, short stories on a topic, and step-by-step directions are especially suited for accordion books. Give accordion books more character by adding an appropriate shape to a file folder accordion book. For example, if students are writing "The Story of Bread," the accordion book could be in the shape of a slice of bread.

**Materials**: manila file folders; 9" x 12" (23 cm x 30 cm) brown construction paper (2 pieces per book); scissors; glue

**Directions (for bread book):** Glue a piece of brown construction paper to the left inside section of an opened folder. Glue a piece of brown construction paper to the right inside section of another opened folder. These will serve as the first and last pages of the book, and represent the "crust" of the bread. Choose an appropriate number of folders for "The Story of Bread." With folders closed, cut a bread slice shape, making sure to leave enough of the fold intact. Arrange the book as shown and tape the folders together. Add a title and ending to the first and last "crust" pages.

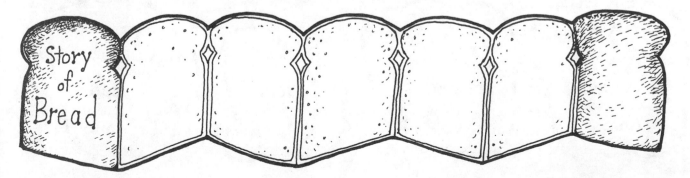

# Rhyme Time!

## Finger Play

**Directions:** Read the poem below. Follow the directions in parentheses ( ) as you read.

*Inside a seed, sound asleep,* (make a fist)
*Lived a little pepper, not making a peep.* (quiet sign)
*Mr. Raindrop knocked on little pepper's door,* (knock)
*"Pitter, pat! Time to do more."* (look at "watch")
*Mrs. Sunbeam sent a message hot,* (arms over head in a circle)
*"Rise and shine! You can give a lot."* (raise arms, frame face and hands)
*The pepper understood;* (shake head "yes")
*Gave a stretch and a yawn;* (stretch and yawn)
*Grew into a pepper, healthy to chew upon.* (eat)

## Rhyming Words

**Directions:** Color the pepper green if it has three rhyming words on it.

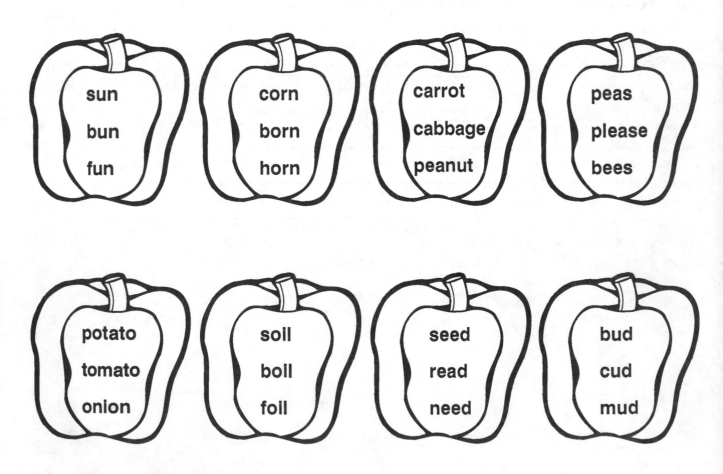

| | | | |
|---|---|---|---|
| sun | corn | carrot | peas |
| bun | born | cabbage | please |
| fun | horn | peanut | bees |

| | | | |
|---|---|---|---|
| potato | soil | seed | bud |
| tomato | boil | read | cud |
| onion | foil | need | mud |

# Tongue Twisters

**Teacher Directions:** Read a few of these food tongue twisters to the students. Have students try reciting them as quickly as they can. Then discuss why these are called tongue twisters. Write some as a class using student names and the names of various foods. Ask students to write and illustrate their own food tongue twisters using the lines below. Detach and assemble students' writing into a class book.

**Peter Piper Picked a Peck of Pickled Peppers.**
**Naughty Nellie Nibbles Noodles Nightly.**
**Brian the Baker Bakes Black Bread.**
**Freddy Fried Fifty Fat Fish.**
**Mary Made Many Marvelous Muffins Monday.**
**Carol Can Crunch Crispy Carrots.**
**Tom Tossed Twenty-Two Tasty Tomatoes.**

_____
*(title)*

_____

_____

_____

_____

_____

by _____

*(picture)*

# From Wheat

**Preparation:** Make copies of game board (pages 44-45) and spinner (page 32). Mount game board on inside of a file folder. Glue directions to front of folder. Provide beans, seeds, unpopped popcorn, etc., as game markers.

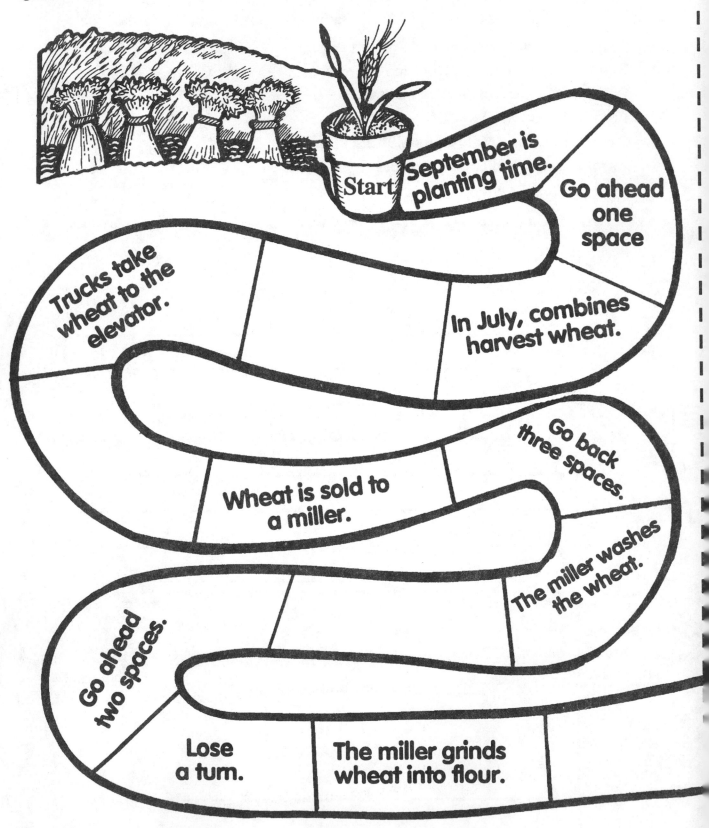

Start — September is planting time.

Go ahead one space

In July, combines harvest wheat.

Trucks take wheat to the elevator.

Go back three spaces.

Wheat is sold to a miller.

The miller washes the wheat.

Go ahead two spaces.

Lose a turn.

The miller grinds wheat into flour.

44

# To Bread

**Directions:** Each player spins the spinner. Player with the highest number goes first. Player 1 spins spinner. He/she must name a word from the game board (or a class list) that begins with one of the blends or digraphs below. To find the blend or digraph to be used in a word, match the spinner number to the number below. (For example, if player spins a 3, he/she must name a word that begins with Br.) If correct, player moves marker the number of spaces indicated by a spin of the spinner. First player to reach bread is the winner.

Spin 1 - Fl    Spin 2 - Tr    Spin 3 - Br    Spin 4 - Wh

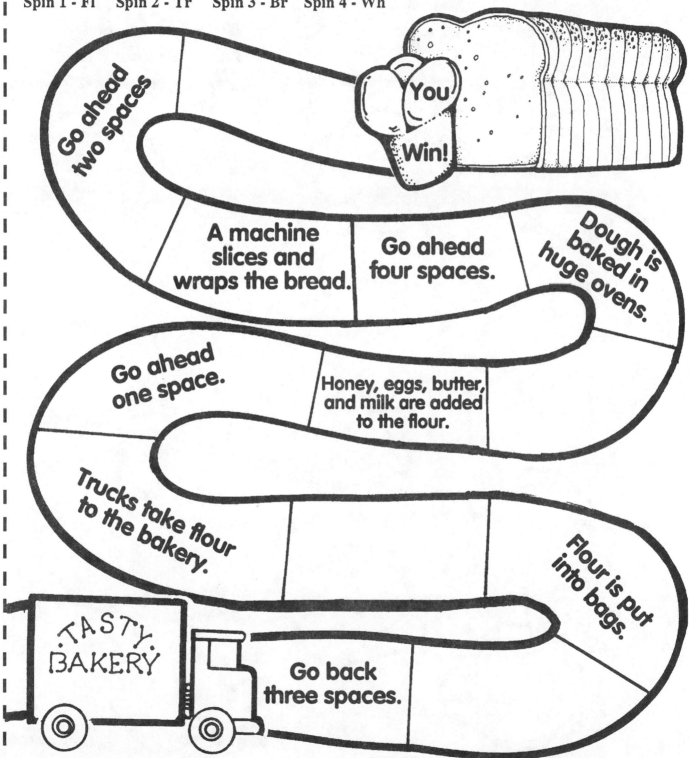

*Math*

**Name** _____

# A-Fishing We Will Go

See page 25 for directions.

**Example**

6 + 2 =

A-fishing we will go.
A-fishing we will go.

We'll catch a fish,
To serve on a dish.
A tasty food you know.

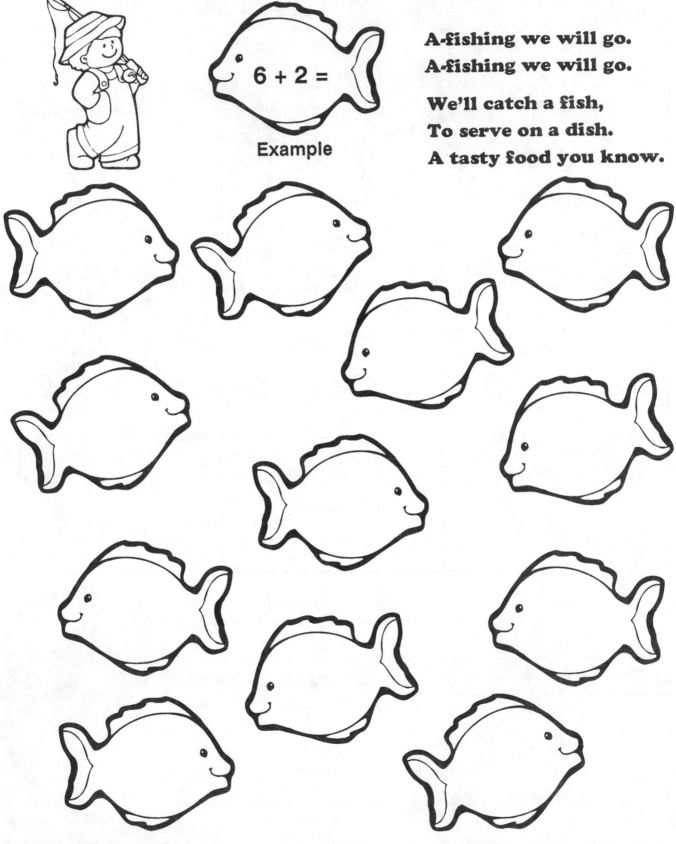

**Name**_____

# Market Street Math

**Directions:** You have just 85 cents to spend on Market Street. You are allowed to buy any two items from the choices below. Can you find two items that you could buy for 85 cents or less? Can you combine another two items? Think of as many combinations of two items as you can. Write the combinations and the cost on the lines below. (An example has been done for you.)

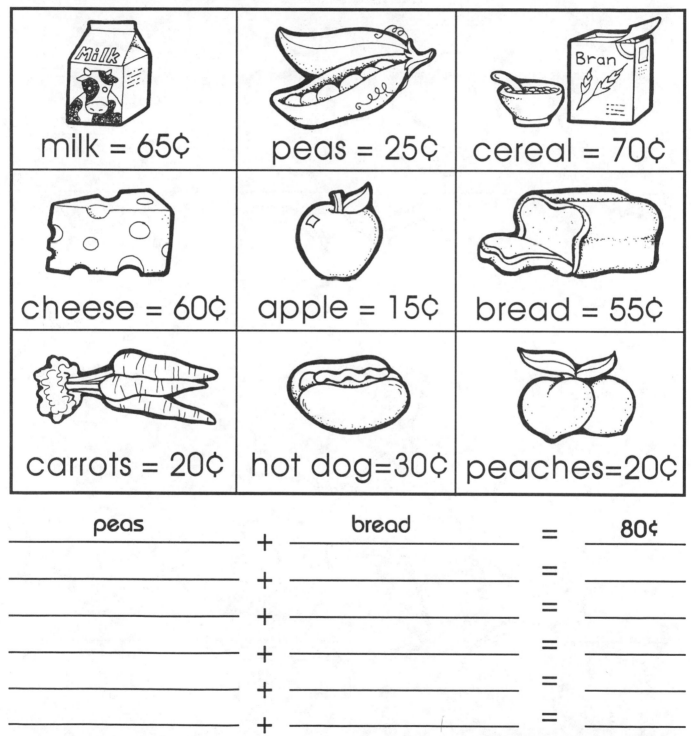

| | | |
|---|---|---|
| milk = 65¢ | peas = 25¢ | cereal = 70¢ |
| cheese = 60¢ | apple = 15¢ | bread = 55¢ |
| carrots = 20¢ | hot dog=30¢ | peaches=20¢ |

peas _____ + _____ bread = ____ 80¢ ____

_____ + _____ = ____

_____ + _____ = ____

_____ + _____ = ____

_____ + _____ = ____

_____ + _____ = ____

_____ + _____ = ____

**Name** _____

# Popcorn Math

**Directions:** Write your own problems in the popcorn flakes below. You may use popped popcorn to help you solve the problems.

     48

# Testing and Tasting Foods

## Growing Bean Sprouts

**Materials**: screw top jar; Mung beans (available from health food store or catalog); screwdriver; water; measuring cup

**Directions**: Measure ½ cup (125 mL) of beans and soak them overnight in cold water. Drain off the water. Punch holes in the jar lid using a screwdriver. Place the beans in the jar and put the lid on. Put the jar in a dark place. Have the students take turns rinsing the beans with water and draining them 2 or 3 times each day. Sprouts grow fast. They should be ready to eat in 5 days. They are good in salads or on sandwiches.

Ask each student to bring a vegetable and make a tossed vegetable "friendship" salad. Let students prepare the Honey Salad Dressing (below) to put on the salad. Don't forget the bean sprouts!

## Honey Salad Dressing

**Ingredients:**

½ cup (125 mL) salad oil

¼ cup (60 mL) vinegar

2 tablespoons (30 mL) soy sauce

1 tablespoon (15 mL) honey

Mix all ingredients in a container. Add salt and pepper. Cover and shake well. Drizzle over vegetable salad.

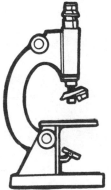

## Under the Microscope

Put a drop of milk on a slide and observe under a microscope. You will see particles floating in a clear liquid. The particles are the fat globules found in milk. Experiment with whole milk, cream, half and half, low-fat milk, and skimmed milk. Compare fat globules.

## Dairy Fat Test

Divide the class into small groups of four or five. Give each group a large brown grocery bag. Provide as many samples of these dairy products as are available: cream, skim milk, sour cream, butter, whole milk, 2 % milk.

Have the students put a small sample of each of the products on the grocery bag and label each one. Allow time for the bag to dry and then examine each spot. Hold it up to the light. Which products allow the most light through? Those contain the most milk fat. Do the findings of each group agree? (Butter, cream, and sour cream contain the most milk fat, followed in order by whole milk, 2% milk, 1% milk, and skim milk.) Compare the results of this fat test to the microscope experiment.

# Where Does Chocolate Come From?

Did you know that chocolate comes from an evergreen tree, called a cacao tree, whose beans (seeds) are used to make all sorts of delicious chocolate treats? The beans are also used to make cocoa butter and medicines. At one time, the people of Mexico and Central America used the cacao bean as a form of money.

Read the information below to find out how chocolate gets from tree to treat!

 1. The cacao tree has many seed pods which grow on stems near the trunk of the tree.

 2. The pods are cut from the branches using long handled knives or machetes.

 3. The beans are then dried to a rich brown color and sent to the factory to be roasted.

 4. Next, the beans are cracked open and the nibs (the edible parts) are separated from the husks.

 5. The nibs are crushed and ground to make liquid chocolate.

 6. Milk and sugar are added and the mixture is blended in big machines called conches.

7. The chocolate is poured into molds and "tapped" to settle it and remove air bubbles.

8. The chocolate is cooled in the molds where it hardens into the tasty treats we like to eat!

# Thank You, Mrs. Pig!

**Directions:** Cut out the wheel. Cut and paste the products on the sections of the wheel. Color and cut out Mrs. Pig (page 52). Cut out the opening on Mrs. Pig. Put the wheel behind Mrs. Pig. Using a brad, poke a hole through the dot on Mrs. Pig and the center of the wheel. Fasten the brad. Tell a story about one or more of the foods that come from Mrs. Pig.

highScience

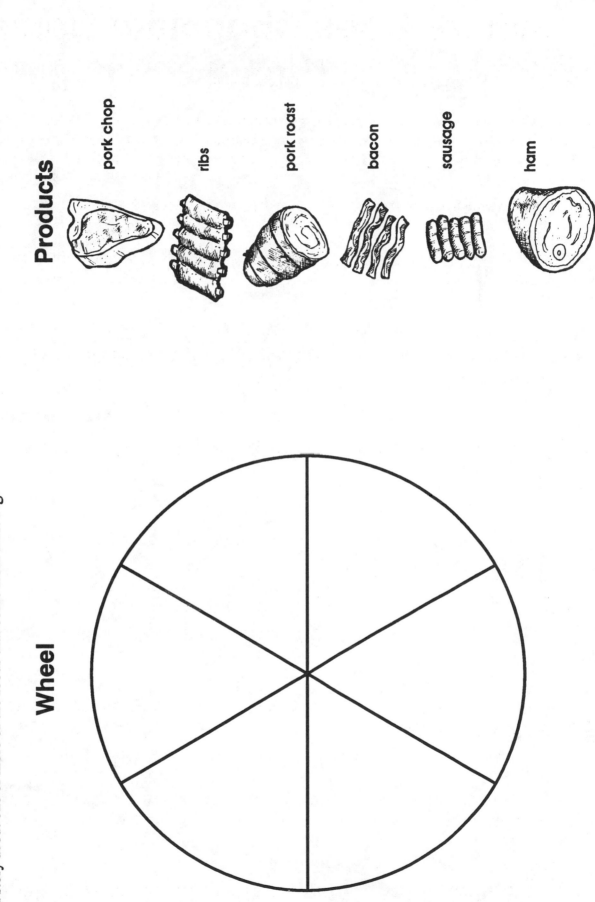

## Products

pork chop

ribs

pork roast

bacon

sausage

ham

## Wheel

# Thank You, Mrs. Pig! *(cont.)*

Cut Out

**Name**_____

# My Five Senses

**Directions:** Think about the different kinds of foods you have tasted, touched, smelled, seen, and even heard! Write some of them on the lines below. Then, compare your food choices with those chosen by classmates.

Five foods I like to **SEE** are:

_____

_____

_____

_____

Five foods I like to **SMELL** are:

_____

_____

_____

_____

Five food sounds I can **HEAR** are:

_____

_____

_____

_____

Five foods that I like to **TOUCH** are:

_____

_____

_____

Five foods I like to **TASTE** are:

_____

_____

_____

_____

# The Busy Bee

**Directions**: Cut out the bees below and paste them in the correct order on the hive on page 55. Make up a "busy bee" story and tell it to a classmate or someone at home.

Beekeeper extracts honey.

Water evaporates from nectar.

Bees fly back to hives.

Bees drink nectar from flowers.

Bees put nectar into honeycombs.

Nectar becomes honey.

- - - - - - - - - - - - - - - - - - - - - - - - - - - - - - - - - - - - - - - -

## Honey of a Story Class Book

**Teacher Directions:** Make two copies of the hive on page 55 using index paper or tag board. (Delete the numbers on the hive first). The hives will serve as front and back covers. Have students press their fingers onto a stamp pad and make fingerprint bees on the front cover (see illustration). Cut lined writing paper in the hive shape and staple the sheets inside the book. Have students write stories about bees and honey, or, list some of the facts they learned about bees.

54

# The Busy Bee (cont.)

See page 54 for directions.

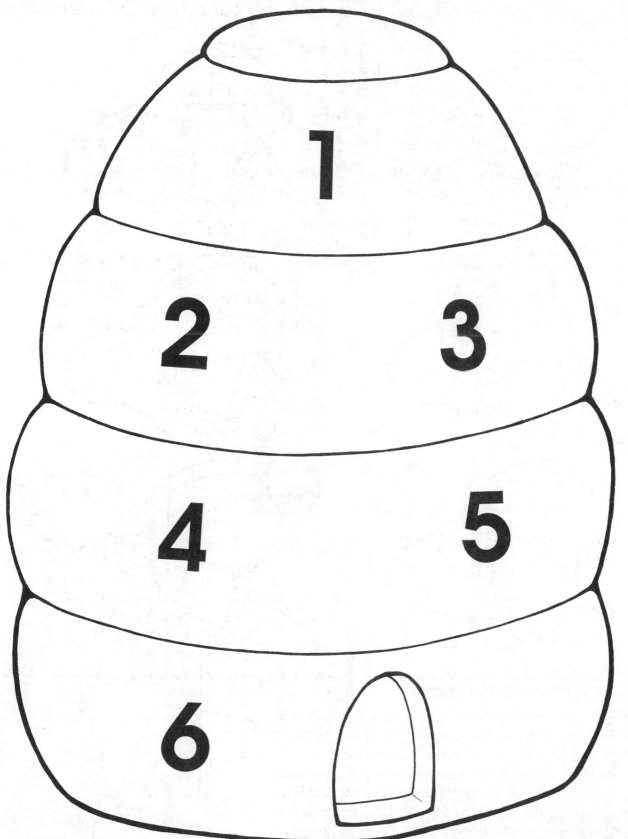

# A Healthy You

You need to eat so you can have energy to work and play. Eating the right foods helps your body grow and stay healthy. The food ingredients your body needs to stay alive and healthy are called nutrients. This chart shows you how foods and their nutrients help you.

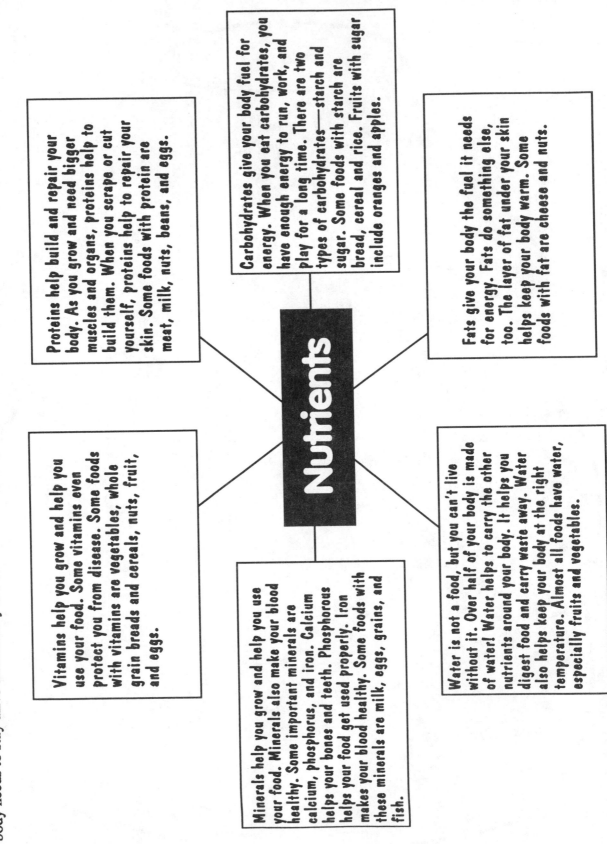

Proteins help build and repair your body. As you grow and need bigger muscles and organs, proteins help to build them. When you scrape or cut yourself, proteins help to repair your skin. Some foods with protein are meat, milk, nuts, beans, and eggs.

Carbohydrates give your body fuel for energy. When you eat carbohydrates, you have enough energy to run, work, and play for a long time. There are two types of carbohydrates— starch and sugar. Some foods with starch are bread, cereal and rice. Fruits with sugar include oranges and apples.

Fats give your body the fuel it needs for energy. Fats do something else, too. The layer of fat under your skin helps keep your body warm. Some foods with fat are cheese and nuts.

**Nutrients**

Vitamins help you grow and help you use your food. Some vitamins even protect you from disease. Some foods with vitamins are vegetables, whole grain breads and cereals, nuts, fruit, and eggs.

Minerals help you grow and help you use your food. Minerals also make your blood healthy. Some important minerals are calcium, phosphorus, and iron. Calcium helps your bones and teeth. Phosphorous helps your food get used properly. Iron makes your blood healthy. Some foods with these minerals are milk, eggs, grains, and fish.

Water is not a food, but you can't live without it. Over half of your body is made of water! Water helps to carry the other nutrients around your body. It helps you digest food and carry waste away. Water also helps keep your body at the right temperature. Almost all foods have water, especially fruits and vegetables.

Name_____

# Fish in the Ocean

**Directions:** Read the poem. Use the sentences that follow to find out how many fish were in each ocean. Draw the correct number of fish in each ocean and label the oceans.

*Fisherman fished in the ocean.*
*Fisherman fished in the sea.*
*Fisherman caught many fish,*
*Will he give some fish to me?*

*He caught one fish in the Arctic Ocean.*
*He caught three fish in the Pacific Ocean.*
*He caught five fish in the Indian Ocean.*
*He caught six fish in the Atlantic Ocean.*

*Fisherman returned with his catch.*
*Fisherman grinned with glee.*
*Fisherman caught quite a batch,*
*And gave them all to me!*

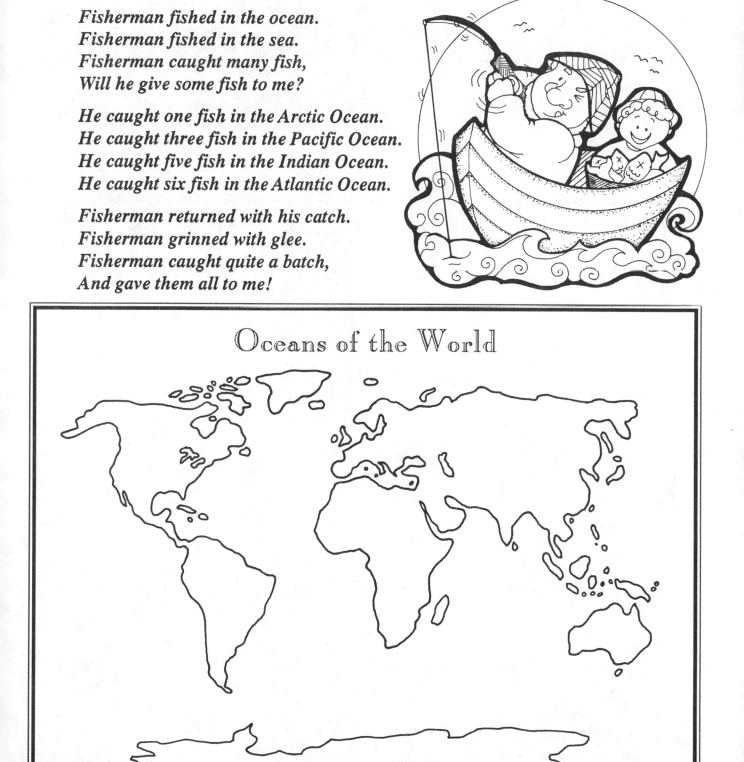

Oceans of the World

# On Which Street?

**Directions**: Locate each store by finding its matching number on the map. Then, on the lines below, write the names of the streets on which the following stores can be found.

Dairy (8) _____    Ice Cream Store (9) _____

Bakery (5) _____    Delicatessen (1) _____

Supermarket (7) _____    Health Food Store (3) _____

Fruit Market (6) _____    Frozen Yogurt Store (10) _____

Pizza Place (2) _____    Hot Dog Stand (4) _____

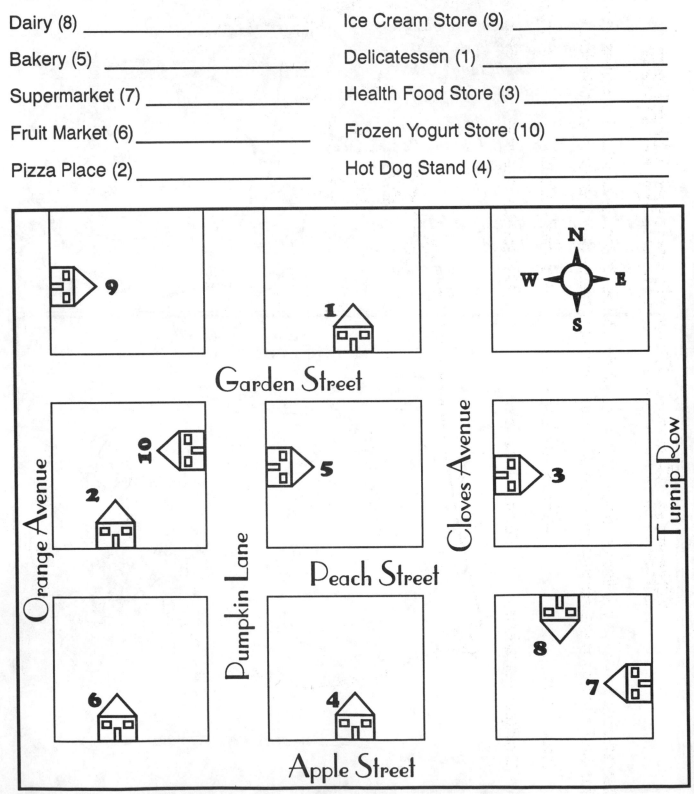

Name

# Some Food Producing States

**Directions:** Locate the following states on a map of the United States. Then label the states on this map and draw the food named on the correct state. Color in the remaining states in one color of your choice.

**Iowa**—corn

**Georgia**—peaches

**Wisconsin**—cheese

**Idaho**—potatoes

**Kansas**—wheat

**California**—oranges

**Washington**—apples

**New Jersey**—tomatoes

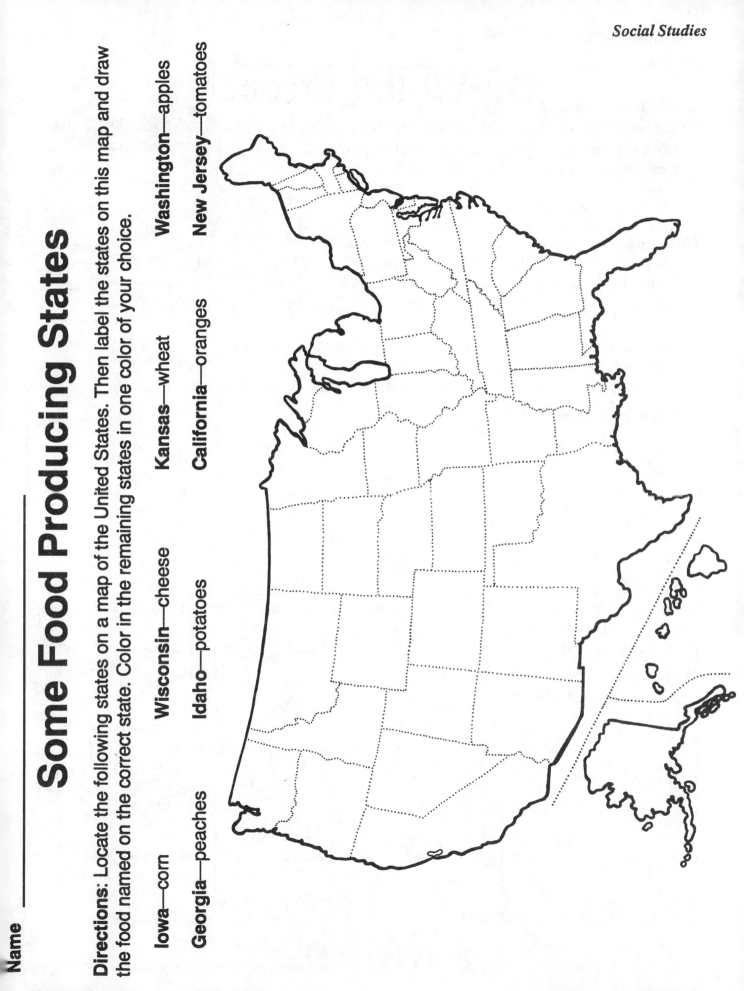

# Tasty Tunes

## Cook Has Put the Soup Pot On

(To the tune of "Polly Put the Kettle On")

*Cook has put the soup pot on, soup pot on, soup pot on.*
*Cook has put the soup pot on, we'll all make soup.*
*(Kevin) put the apples in, apples in, apples in.*
*(Kevin) put the apples in, we'll all stir the soup.*
*(Manuela) put the broccoli in, broccoli in, broccoli in.*
*(Manuela) put the broccoli in, we'll all stir the soup.*
*(Susan) put the carrots in, carrots in, carrots in.*
*(Susan) put the carrots in, we'll all stir the soup.*

(Proceed through the alphabet with each student adding a food beginning with the next letter of the alphabet.)

Place a large pan at the front of the group and have students act out placing the food in the pot. After they have placed their "food" in the pot, they should stay and help with the "stirring" each time. You should end up with a large circle of students standing around the pot, "stirring."

## Oats, Peas, Beans and Barley Grow

*Oats, Peas, Beans and Barley Grow;*
*Oats, Peas, Beans and Barley Grow;*
*Can you or I or anyone know*
*How Oats, Peas, Beans and Barley Grow?*

_____, _____, _____ and _____ Grow;
_____, _____, _____ and _____ Grow;

*Can you or I or anyone know*
*How* _____, _____, _____ and _____ Grow?

Discuss syllables. Have the students suggest other foods of one syllable for the first three blanks and two syllable food words for the last blank in each line.

## Old McDonald Had a Cow

(To the tune of "Old McDonald Had a Farm")

*Old McDonald had a cow, A-E-I-O-U.*
*And from that cow he got some milk, A-E-I-O-U.*
*With a pint, pint here, and a quart, quart there,*
*Here a pint, there a quart, everywhere a gal-lon,*
*Old McDonald had a cow, A-E-I-O-U!*

(Rewrite for pig, fish pond, hive, chicken, etc.)

## Popcorn

(To the tune of "Pop Goes the Weasel")

*All around the popcorn pan,*
*The kernels jump and sizzle.*
*Hold the lid on tight if you can.*
*Pop, goes the popcorn!*

60

# Food Games

## A Very Filling Sandwich

Two "slices of bread" (students) stand facing each other about two feet apart. The remainder of the children form a line and walk between the sandwich. The group sings the song below to the tune of "London Bridge." The child in the middle must name a filling and its source after the word "with" (at the end of the verse).

> (To the tune of "London Bridge")
> *Our Sandwich is filling up, filling up, filling up.*
> *Our Sandwich is filling up with_____.*

**Examples:**

> *Our sandwich is filling up with* (tomatoes from the garden).
> *Our sandwich is filling up with* (tuna from the ocean).
> *Our sandwich is filling up with* (honey from the bees).

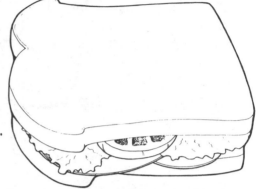

After each child has named a filling he/she stays between the bread and the song begins again until everyone has become the "filling" and the sandwich is big enough for a giant.

## Onion Run

Children sit in a large circle on the floor. The "gardener" walks around the outside of the circle tapping each child on the head and naming plant foods, such as carrots, cabbage, tomatoes, celery, grapes, oranges, or onions . Whenever the gardener says "onion", that child jumps up and runs around the circle trying to get back to the empty space before the gardener. During the chase the group chants "Run, Onion, Run." If the onion loses the race everyone stands and cries "Boo-hoo." The group returns to a sitting position and the onion becomes the gardener.

## You Can Do It!

Use two clean fruit or vegetable cans. Put a ping-pong ball in one can. Flip the ping-pong ball over your head and try to catch it in the other can. Set the timer. See who can catch it the most times in the allotted time.

## Can You Win?

Using two tall metal juice cans, make a pair of stilts. Cut the bottom out of both cans and punch two holes across from each other in the top end. Thread a rope or twine through the holes leaving ends long enough for students to hold onto when standing on the juice cans. Make several pairs and have "giant" relays.

## Container Catch

Using empty gallon milk jugs, cut away part of the bottom section (see diagram). Use soft foam balls or bean bags to play catch between two or more students. (Students hold container upside-down by handle and try to scoop the ball or bean bag into the container.)

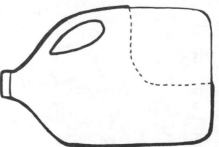

# Desk Top Story Starter

**Directions:** Cut out the cow patterns. Color the areas marked 'C' with a black crayon. Fold the cow's body along the dashed lines. Using scissors, cut along the dashed lines at the top of the cow's head and curl toward the eyes with a pencil. Using tape or glue, attach the head and tail tabs to the tab markings on the body of the cow.

tab
A

tab
B
C

tab
A

tab
B

C

C

C

C

C

C

C

C

# A Mooo-ving Cow

**Directions:** Color and cut out the barn and cow patterns. Punch holes through the black dots. Thread yarn through the holes as shown below. Tie the yarn ends together near the center back of the picture. "Moooooove" the cow to the barn.

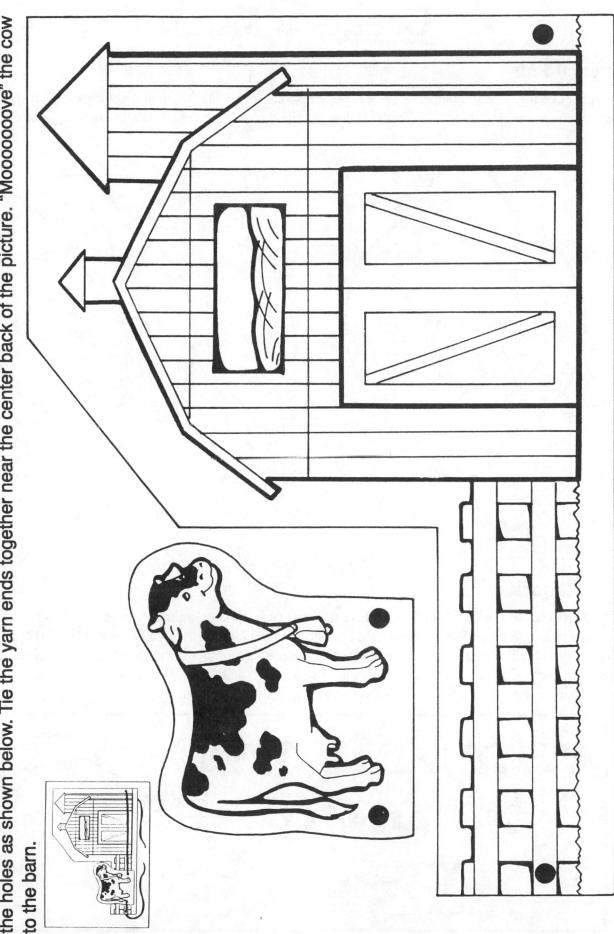

# Create a Moood!

## Pencil Pals

Reproduce these pencil pals on heavy paper. Have students color them and cut the patterns out. Cut small slashes where indicated. Students slip pencils through the pencil pals to create a "mooood" for writing.

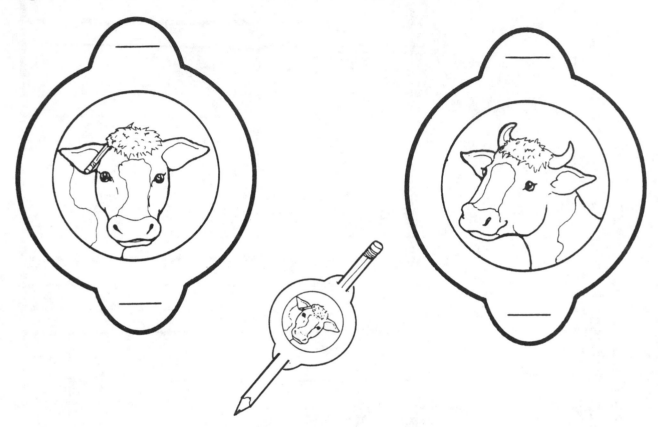

## Bookmark

Make copies of the cow bookmark. Have students color the bookmarks. Cover just the front of the bookmark with clear contact paper. Punch a hole where indicated. Give students three 10" (25 cm) pieces of black or white yarn. Have them pull the pieces together through the hole so that the yarn is even on both sides of the hole. Tie the yarn in a knot at the hole to form a tail. Use the back to list new or difficult words, or interesting facts learned while studying about the milk makers.

64

# What's Cookin'?

## Homemade Butter

Long ago, people made butter in a butter churn. Today it is made in large drums at a creamery. Students can share in this fascinating process with the following activity.

Place one cup (250 mL) of heavy whipping cream (room temperature) in a small jar with a tight fitting lid. Add one clean marble. Screw the lid on tightly and take turns shaking vigorously for about ten minutes. The tiny, round globules of fat in the cream are forced to stick together to make butter. Drain the buttermilk and taste it. Press the butter pieces together and rinse the butter several times with cold water. Work a little salt into the butter and sample it on a cracker.

## A Green Sandwich

Slice large cucumbers so each student has two slices. Put one tablespoon (15 mL) of cottage cheese between the two slices and enjoy a healthy sandwich.

## Yeast Fungus

Explain to students that yeast is very often used in bread to make it rise. Let students experience how yeast works by dissolving some in lukewarm water and "feeding" it some honey. They will soon observe a bubbly foam on top of the mixture. The chemical reaction causes yeast to give off carbon dioxide and alcohol. The trapped carbon dioxide is what causes bread to rise. Choose a favorite yeast bread recipe to make and enjoy in class.

## Tangy Orange Juice

Using a juicy valencia orange, cut a tiny hole and insert a plastic straw. Squeeze the orange and enjoy the juice from its natural source.

## Magic Cow Floats

Mix the following ingredients together and pour into glasses:

1 package pre-sweetened fruit flavored drink mix

2 $1/3$ cups (625 mL) non-fat dry milk

2 quarts (2 L) cold water

To each glass, add a small scoop of ice cream and a straw and enjoy your Magic Cow Float.

## Curds and Whey (Cottage Cheese)

Pour 2 cups (500 mL) of milk into a saucepan. Add 3 tablespoons (45 mL) of vinegar or lemon juice. Put saucepan on low heat and stir slowly for about 8 minutes. When curds begin to form, remove from heat and continue stirring. When all curdling stops, pour mixture into a bowl and refrigerate until cool. Add salt or sugar if desired. If curds are drained well and cream added, you will have cottage cheese.

Name _____

# Comparing Labels

**Directions:** Compare two cereal boxes from your cupboard at home or from the supermarket shelf. Then, fill in the lines on Box A and Box B with the information from your cereal boxes. Illustrate and color a sample of your cereal at the bottom of each box.

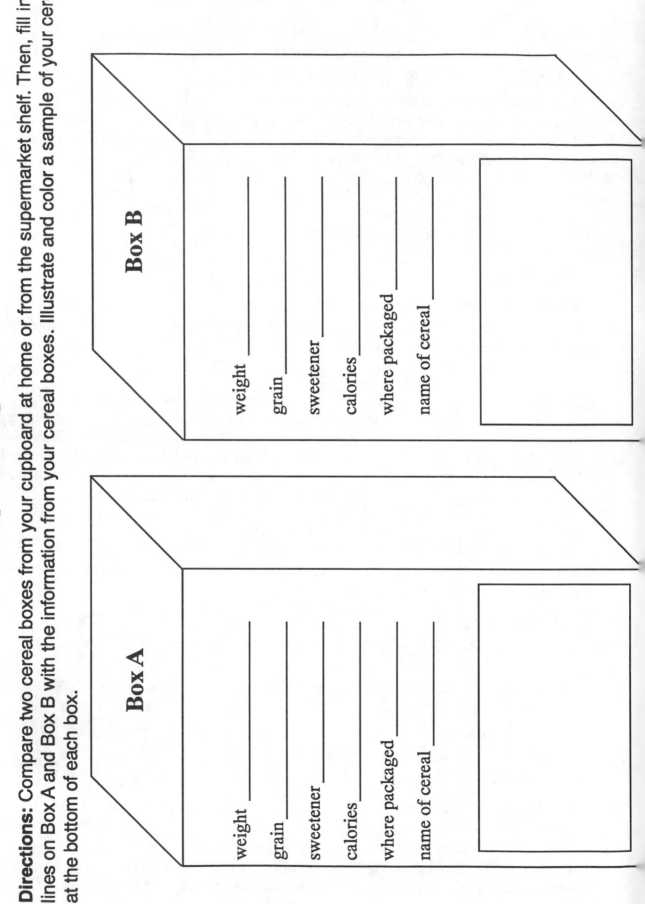

## Box A

weight _____

grain _____

sweetener _____

calories _____

where packaged _____

name of cereal _____

## Box B

weight _____

grain _____

sweetener _____

calories _____

where packaged _____

name of cereal _____

66

# Food Fun Day

The purpose of the Food Fun Day is for children to share with others the activities and learning experiences they encountered throughout the thematic unit.

- Foster student ownership in the Food Fun Day by allowing students to choose which activities they would like to present in addition to your general outline of events.

- Plan the day's activities with the children. Prepare the room for guests. Have students fill out and send the invitations on page 75. Practice the songs, poems, and games presented in the unit and have students practice the Readers' Theater play on pages 21 and 22.

- Decide which foods will be prepared for the Food Fun Day. You may want to include foods from all food groups and have a student presentation about the Food Pyramid and the need for a balanced diet. Set up tables for eating and cooking and decide how and when each activity will take place. (Students may wish to make a class recipe book to give to guests.)

- Allow the students to act as hosts and hostesses by showing guests the student-authored products displayed around the room. Be sure to include a visit to the activity centers (pages 69-73).

- Prepare the awards on page 74 and present them to students as part of the Food Fun Day. Be sure that each child has the opportunity to participate in some way during the day's activities. This event should be an enjoyable and rewarding culmination of your unit on food.

# Activity Centers

Activity Centers are stations for individual and group learning. They consist of spaces (tables, counter tops, even hanging wall displays) where activities are arrayed for use by the students. These activities usually deal with a single concept or a project such as research, writing, art, or science, and contain some hands-on materials.

Activity Centers provide a good opportunity for cooperative learning and enhance the learning of social skills. They are appealing to students because they accommodate a variety of learning styles and promote individual (or group) accomplishment. Creativity and critical thinking skills are encouraged through hands-on manipulation of materials.

An activity center can be used every day or just 2 or 3 days a week. Some teachers prefer to use centers four days a week and culminate with a special activity on Friday.

## Organizing the Classroom for Learning Centers

Divide the class into manageable groups of five or six students. Give each group a name or letter. Students do not need to be ability grouped but try to inconspicuously provide a leader for each group. Designate a table or floor space for the center. Label and make certain enough supplies are available. Provide a model of the finished product if possible. It will cut down on the number of interruptions during your small group time.

Cut out a shape, like Mr. Tomato Man (right), and attach it with a paper fastener to a chart that has been divided into the day's activities. Establish an appropriate number of minutes for students to work at a center before moving on to the next activity. If students are not finished with their projects have them attach all the parts together and place projects in a specified area. Allow time at the end of the day for finishing up the day's work or reading.

## Center Suggestions for This Unit

- **Liquid Measurement**

   Cover a work area with a large bath or beach towel to catch any small spills. Provide a cup, pint, quart, half gallon and gallon milk container. Label each one with a permanent marker. Have students use water to become familiar with liquid measures, make comparisons, and find equivalent measures.

- **Linear Measurement**

   Bring carrots, cucumbers, green beans, and celery to class for a measurement center. Supply rulers or yarn and have students measure the length of each food. Ask students to draw each vegetable on paper and record the length. Using a 2 pound (1 kg) bag of carrots, ask students to arrange the carrots from shortest to longest.

# Activity Centers *(cont.)*

## Center Suggestions for This Unit *(cont.)*

* **Weighing Produce**

  Place a variety of foods at a center. Give each food a name and label. Have students place foods on a scale, one at a time. Make copies of the face of the scale and ask students to draw the hand of the scale pointing to the closest number on the actual scale.

* **Food Pyramid**

  Bring in empty, clean containers, packages, boxes, etc., of products. If possible, bring in real fruits, vegetables, breads, etc. (Or, mount pictures of foods on pieces of construction paper.) Prepare a large model of the Food Pyramid (see page 11) on tag board or poster board. Have students place the correct amount of food on each section of the pyramid.

* **Count the Seeds**

  Have a student bring in a pumpkin, a pepper, or an ear of dried corn. Let the students count and record the number of seeds found in each. Incorporate math concepts by asking students to group by tens, estimate, and solve problems using the seeds as manipulatives.

* **Supermarket**

  Ask the students to bring in clean, empty food cans and boxes. Label them with a price appropriate for your grade level. Use a toy cash register and play money for shopping. Students should be given an appropriate amount of play money and allowed to "shop." Depending on grade level, the teacher may need to be the cashier to demonstrate the proper counting of change.

* **Refrigerator Magnets**

  Trim crust from white bread (use crust as animal food). Tear the bread into small pieces. Add white glue (8 slices of bread to $^1/_2$ cup/125 mL glue) and knead until smooth. Shape into a vegetable to be used as a refrigerator magnet. Let dry overnight on waxed paper. Paint and attach a small magnet strip with a glue gun.

* **Vegetable Quilt**

  Using Lois Ehlert's collage technique, have each student cut out a favorite vegetable and glue it to a 6" x 6" (15 cm x 15 cm) piece of white tag board. Mark five equidistant X's, $^1/_2$" (1 cm) in from each side of the square. Punch holes on the X's. Let students join their squares together with yarn to make a "Colorful Garden Quilt."

* **Bag It**

  Cut out pictures of foods from all food groups represented in the Food Pyramid. Glue them to construction paper. Laminate, if possible, for greater durability. Cut out the patterns on pages 71-73 and staple or glue each to a grocery bag.

  Place all the pictures in a container at a center. Ask students to sort food items into the correct food category.

  **Note:** Patterns may be used for bulletin boards or wall displays, too.

# Activity Centers *(cont.)*

## Center Suggestions for This Unit *(cont.)*

• **Potato Prints**
   Cut potatoes in half so each student has one half. Using a marker or pencil, have them draw a design on the cut side of the potato. With a paring knife or their scissors students can cut away the part (about ¼"/1.6 cm deep) that is not the design. (This activity needs supervision.) Provide tempera paint and a large brush for them to paint over the face of their design. They can then stamp their design around the edge of a sheet of paper to make a border for a picture or writing activity.

• **Poetry Paddles**
   Have students copy a food poem on a 3" x 5" (8 cm x 13 cm) blank index card (put the 3" side at the top). On another card of the same size (turned the same way) have students illustrate the poem. Glue or staple the cards to the front and back of a tongue depressor to create a poetry paddle to share with their family and friends.

• **Pocket Folder Fun**
   Duplicate several pictures of broccoli heads and stems. Put a picture of a word representing a blend (old workbooks are good sources for pictures) on the broccoli head and write the word on the stem, highlighting the blend sound. Illustrate the cover of a pocket folder and label the inside pockets as shown. Place heads and stems in folder. Students, in pairs or individually, match the words and pictures that have the same beginning blends. (You can adapt this activity as a matching game to reinforce other skills.)

• **Counting Coins**
   Trucks bring us many of our foods. Trucks make it possible to enjoy foods out of season.

   Make several copies of a truck pattern (see example). Place them in an activity center. Write an amount of money on the front wheel and stamp coins on the two rear wheels equal to that amount. Students join the cab of the truck to the trailer at the black dot with a paper fastener. Extending the back bumper would allow an additional trailer with coins in the correct amount to be joined. Provide supplies and money stamps so children can make and decorate a truck of their own when finished at the center.

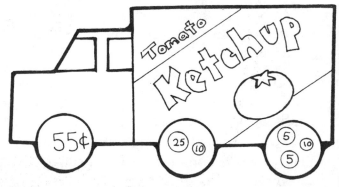

# Activity Center Patterns

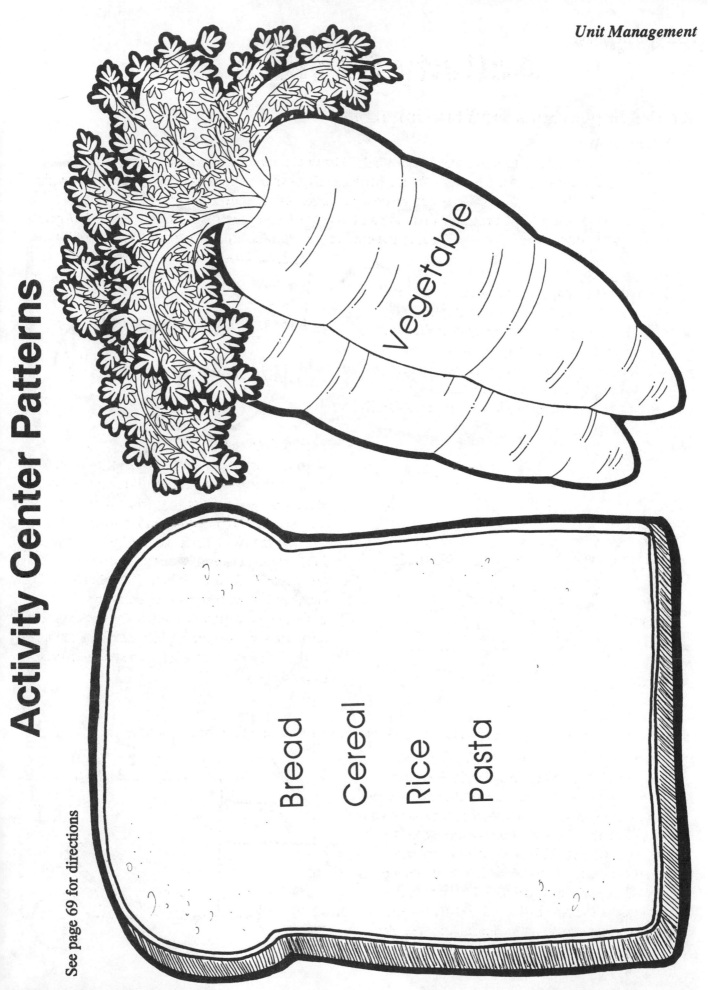

Vegetable

Bread

Cereal

Rice

Pasta

See page 69 for directions

# Activity Center Patterns (cont.)

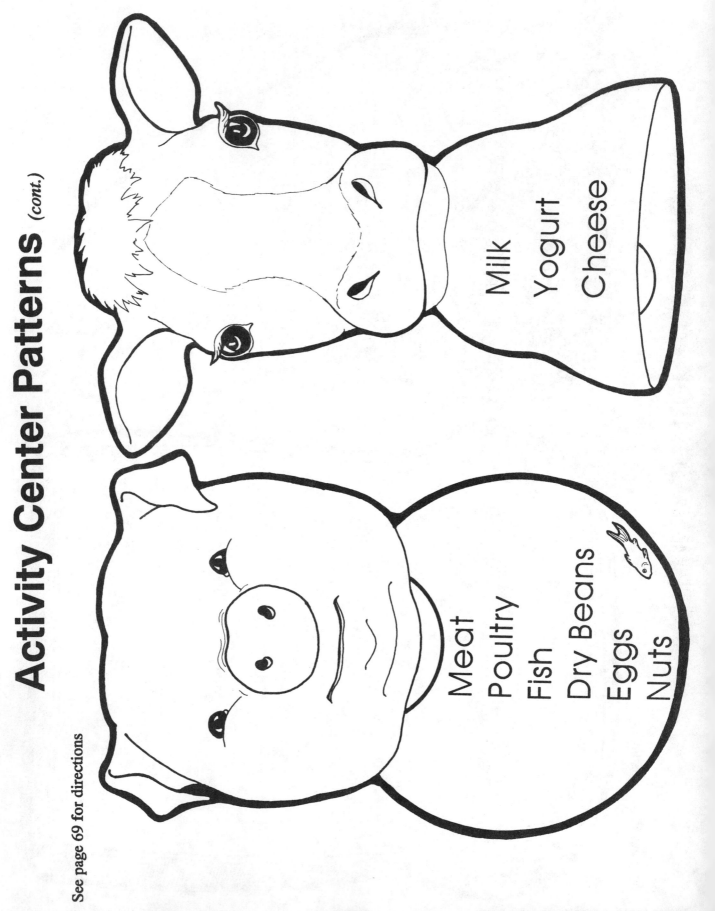

Milk
Yogurt
Cheese

Meat
Poultry
Fish
Dry Beans
Eggs
Nuts

See page 69 for directions

72

# Activity Center Patterns *(cont.)*

Fruit

Fats Oils Sweets

CORN OIL

See page 69 for directions

# Awards

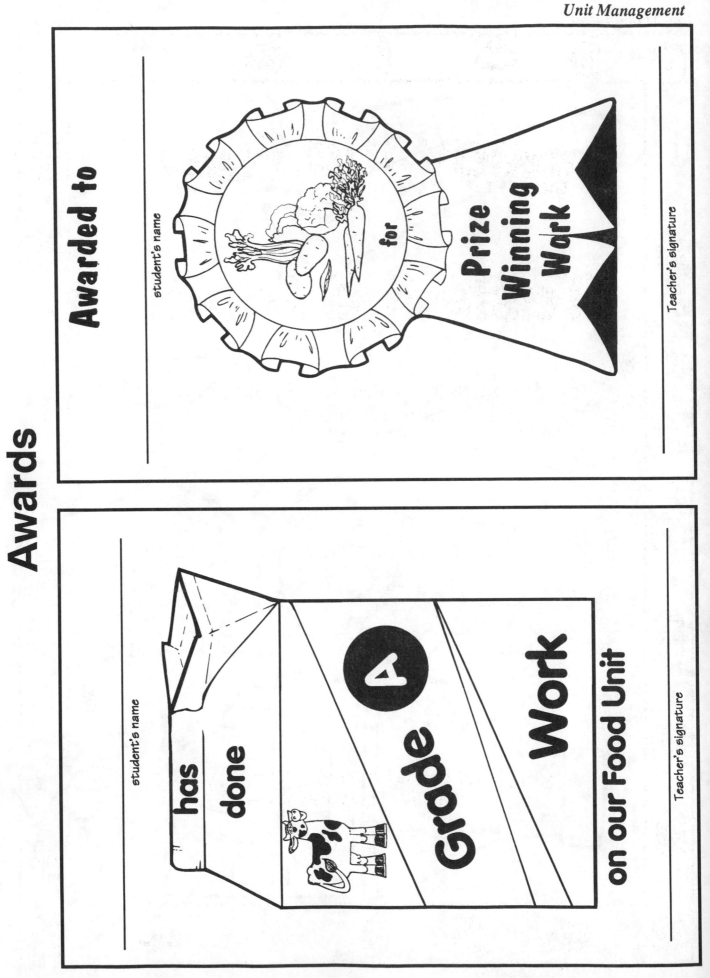

Awarded to

_____
student's name

for

Prize Winning Work

_____
Teacher's signature

_____
student's name

has done

Grade A

Work

on our Food Unit

_____
Teacher's signature

# Enjoy the Fun!

# Taste the Food!

You are cordially invited to join our class for a Food Fun Day.

Date: _____

Time: _____

Place: _____

Bring your appetite and get ready for a deliciously good time.

# Bulletin Board

Use the following interactive bulletin board to enhance the unit and encourage students to expand their knowledge of food products and healthy eating habits.

## From Our Garden

**Directions**: As a background, attach blue butcher paper or construction paper to a bulletin board or wall. Add a food theme border, if possible. Put strips of brown paper (three different shades) along the bottom of the display. Have students cut vegetables from brightly colored paper to "plant" in the garden. Label vegetables using tongue depressors.

## Extensions:

1. Have each student write a few sentences, a poem, an acrostic, etc., about the vegetable on an index card and attach it next to the vegetable.

2. Have students use the three levels (brown paper strips) to illustrate vegetables we eat that come from roots, stems, and leaves, or flowers.

3. Use the same bulletin board idea for fruits by creating an orchard background.

# Field Trip

See page 8 for directions.

## Supermarket Search

Name _____ Team _____

| Fruit or Vegetable | Canned | Frozen | Fresh |
|---|---|---|---|
| | | | |
| | | | |
| | | | |
| | | | |
| | | | |
| | | | |
| | | | |
| | | | |
| | | | |

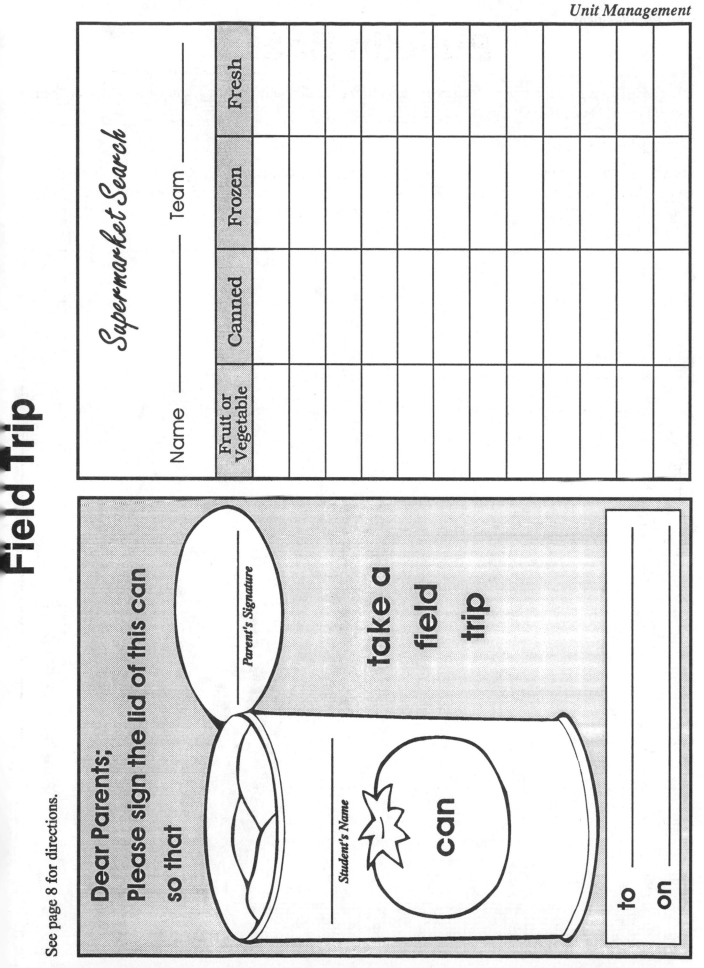

Dear Parents;
Please sign the lid of this can

so that

*Parent's Signature*

*Student's Name*

can

take a
field
trip

to _____

on _____

# Answer Key

**Page 10**

**Fruit**

tomato

green bean

zucchini

peppers

**Roots**

carrots

**Seeds**

corn

peas

**Tuber**

potato

onion

**Leaves**

cabbage

**Flower**

broccoli

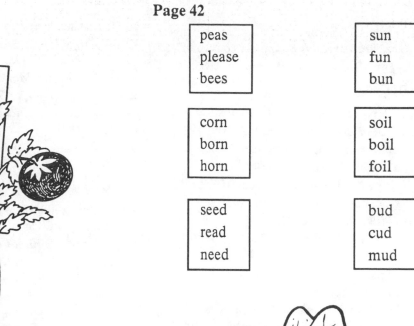

**Page 14**

One sunny day, Mrs. Crunch gathered red juicy **tomatoes** from her garden, crunchy, orange **carrots** from her garden, leafy, green **lettuce** from her garden, round, white **onions** from her garden, and sweet, green **peppers** from her garden. Then she said, "I will ask all my friends to come for lunch. It will be ready in fifteen minutes."

Mrs. Crunch and her friends will have a salad.

**Page 31**

pasteurized

rennet

curds

whey

heated

knives

salt

cheese

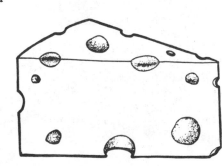

**Page 42**

| peas | | sun |
| please | | fun |
| bees | | bun |

| corn | | soil |
| born | | boil |
| horn | | foil |

| seed | | bud |
| read | | cud |
| need | | mud |

**Page 55**

1. Bees drink nectar from flowers.
2. Bees fly back to their hives.
3. Bees put nectar into honeycombs.
4. Water evaporates from the nectar.
5. The nectar becomes honey.
6. Beekeeper extracts the honey.

**Page 58**

Dairy- Peach Street

Bakery- Pumpkin Lane

Supermarket-Turnip Row

Fruit Market- Apple Street

Pizza Place-Peach Street

Ice Cream Store- Orange Avenue

Delicatessen- Garden Street

Health Food Store- Cloves Avenue

Frozen Yogurt Store- Pumpkin Lane

Hot Dog Stand- Apple Street

# Bibliography & Resources

## Core Books

Ehlert, Lois. *Growing Vegetable Soup.* Harcourt, 1987.

Gibbons, Gail. *The Milk Makers.* Macmillan, 1985.

## Nonfiction

Aliki. *Green Grass and White Milk.* Crowell, 1974.

Althea. *Where Does Food Come From?* Rourke, 1981.

Ancona, George. *Bananas.* Clarion Books, 1982.

Carrick, Donald. *Milk.* Greenwillow, 1985.

Ehlert, Lois. *Eating the Alphabet.* Harcourt, 1989.

___ *Food Works.* Ontario Science Centre, 1987

Gregory, O. B. *Milk.* Rourke, 1981.

Kalman, Bobbie. *The Food We Eat.* Crabtree, 1986.

Kelley, True. *Let's Eat!* E. P. Dutton, 1986.

McFarland, Cynthia. *Cows in the Parlor.* Atheneum, 1990.

McMillan, Bruce. *Growing Colors.* Lothrop, 1988.

Mitgutsch, Ali. *From Beet to Sugar.* Carolrhoda, 1981.
  *From Blossom to Honey.* Carolrhoda, 1981.
  *From Grass to Butter.* Carolrhoda, 1981.

Moncure, Jane Belk. *What Was It Before It Was Bread?* Child's World, 1985.
  *What Was It Before It Was Orange Juice?* Child's World, 1985.

Oechsli, Helen. *In My Garden: A Child's Gardening Book.* Macmillan, 1985.

Patent, Dorothy Hinshaw. *A Picture Book of Cows.* Holiday House, 1982.

Riece, Coleen. *What Was It Before It Was Ice Cream?* Child's World, 1985.

Rogow, Zack. *Oranges.* Franklin Watts, 1988.

Steele, Mary Q. *Anna's Garden Songs.* Scholastic, 1989.

Turner, Dorothy. *Bread.* Carolrhoda, 1989.
  *Milk.* Carolrhoda, 1989.

## Fiction

Balian, Lorna. *A Garden for a Groundhog.* Humbug Press, 1985.

Bunting, Eve. *The Big Cheese.* Macmillan, 1977.

Burningham, John. *The Shopping Basket.* Crowell, 1980.

Carle, Eric. *Pancakes, Pancakes.* Picture Book Studio, 1990.

de Paola, Tomie. *The Popcorn Book.* Holiday House, 1978.
  *Strega Nona.* Simon & Schuster, 1975.
  *Watch Out for Chicken Feet in Your Soup.* Prentice Hall, 1974.

Domanska, Janina. *The Little Red Hen.* Macmillan, 1973.

Ernst, Lisa Campbell. *Miss Penny and Mr. Grubbs.* Bradbury Press, 1991.

Hurd, Thacher. *The Pea Patch Jig.* Crown, 1986.

Khalsa, Dayal Kaur. *How Pizza Came to Queens.* C. N. Potter, 1989.

Lobel, Arnold. *On Market Street.* Greenwillow, 1981.

Root, Phyllis. *Soup for Supper.* Harper & Row, 1986.

Sendak, Maurice. *Chicken Soup With Rice.* Harper & Row, 1962.

Westcott, Nadine. *The Giant Vegetable Garden.* Little, Brown, 1981.

## Cookbooks for Kids

*Better Homes and Gardens Step-by-Step Kids' Cookbook.* Better Homes and Gardens, 1984.

Coyle, Rena. *My First Baking Book.* Workman, 1988.

Coyle, Rena. *My First Cookbook.* Workman, 1985.

Gibbons, Gail. *The too-great bread bake book.* Warner, 1980.

O'Connor, Jane. *The Care Bear's party cook book.* Random House, 1985.

Watson, N. Cameron. *The Little Pigs' First Cookbook.* Little, 1987.

Zweifel, Frances. *Pickle in the Middle and Other Easy Snacks.* Harper, 1979.

## Resources

Write to the following for more information on:

**Bread:**

Fleishman's Yeast
P.O. Box 7004
San Francisco, CA 94120-7004

**Canning:**

Owatonna Canning Co.
P. O. Box 447
Owatonna, MN 55060-0447

**Ketchup:**

Heinz U.S.A.
600 Grant St.
P. O. Box 57
Pittsburgh, PA 15230
*(Ask for the story of ketchup)*

**Cereal:**

Kellogg Co.
180 South Union
Battle Creek, MI 49017

**Dairy Products:**

National Dairy Council
6300 North River Rd.
Rosemont, IL 60018